KEEPING
COMPANY
WITH JESUS

KEEPING
COMPANY
WITH JESUS

Reflections on Gospel Stories

Jackie L. Smallbones

Augsburg Books
MINNEAPOLIS

CONTENTS

To Mom and Dad,
who first introduced me to Gospel stories,
then taught me to love the One to whom they point

FOREWORD

How do we capture the essence of who Jesus was and is? What metaphor can describe him and his ministry? Ted Loder uses the metaphor of "Guerrillas of Grace" to describe the lives of believers as they reflect on the ministry of Jesus. Clarence Jordan spoke of Jesus as a "compassionate radical." At times Jesus has been spoken of as a "subversive" (Luke 23:2). Each of these images seeks to present him as one who opposes the status quo in gentle, yet powerful ways. His message and actions were such that the Jewish leaders saw him as a direct threat to their position of authority, but the common people who grew close to him found him to be one who brought liberation from religious bondage and taught them that they could call God *Father*.

If Jesus had taught his message overtly and directly, he would have been challenged and perhaps even immediately arrested by the Jewish religious leaders. Moreover, the attacks by the religious leaders would have been even more severe.

But he was too wise to launch a frontal attack. He used a subversive approach that disarmed opponents and reduced opposition. His teaching and actions were, for the most part, subtle and nuanced. People had to think about what he did and said for some time in order to catch the full meaning of his message.

Many of Jesus's parables were directed against the religious establishment. If he proclaimed his message directly, there would have been severe consequences, as it so undermined the authority of the leaders. But his parables were like a Trojan horse, seemingly innocent, until they were "unpacked," and their full meaning understood, by which time he had moved on and the leaders were left to face the implications of what he had said.

Jesus spoke out, not only against the "establishment," but also against individual lives. His teaching revolutionizes the status quo of our lives, if we take the time to listen. It is dangerous stuff that forces us to look deep inside ourselves and face our own prejudices, our pride, and our assumptions. If we really listen, we have to reconstruct our understanding of ourselves, the world around us, and of God and God's relationship to creation. Jesus's followers were known as people who "have been turning the world upside down" (Acts 17:6) because they were taking his teaching seriously. Indeed, in the paradoxical topography of the kingdom of God as proclaimed by Jesus, the way "up" is "down" (Mark 10:44).

Part of the key to really listening is to watch as well as listen. We must watch what Jesus *did,* and listen to what he *taught* (Acts 1:1). Because so much of his teaching was subtle, we need to spend time with him—watching, listening, and thinking. Through what he did and did not do, Jesus subverted the culture of his day and the lives of the people he encountered. His subversion was not only to tear down, but also to build up. He replaced old, erroneous assumptions with a new vision of the kingdom, where peace and justice rule and where God is honored in spirit and in truth.

If we are serious about keeping company with Jesus, there are two necessary prerequisites. The first is a willingness to change. The penetrating question to the man who had been ill for thirty-eight years is the question we too must face: "Do you want to be made well?" (John 5:6). If we enjoy life as it is, with a comfortable faith that is not disruptive but only affirming, then it is not wise to keep company with Jesus. Engaging God in the way that Jesus proclaimed brings healing, but it also brings unforeseen challenges to our comfortable lives. We must be willing to let a prophet enter our homes and speak the truth in love. It is dangerous to keep company with a prophet.

The second prerequisite is that we must come hungering and thirsting after righteousness, being willing to seek first the kingdom of God. Mary reminds us that God "has filled the hungry with good things, and sent the rich away empty" (Luke 1:53). Jesus has the disruptive, subversive, nurturing, and healing words of life. At the end of the day, when our lives have been confronted, our assumptions challenged, and our values examined, we discover that his yoke is easy and his burden is light.

Jackie Smallbones invites us into a journey with her as she brings us face to face with Jesus. Her life has been one of contemplation, reflection, and honesty. We were privileged to be her hosts during part of her extensive period of unemployment. We were able to watch and listen as she kept company with Jesus during this dark period in her life. She offers the self-revelation of one who has struggled to understand. But more important, she offers insights into the one who is the way, the truth, and the life. Keeping company with Jesus is a dangerous practice because of what it will do to us. Yet it is also the way of life. We invite you to walk with Jesus and listen as Jackie shares her observations along the way.

Perry and Sandy Downs

Perry is associate dean for doctoral programs at Trinity Evangelical Divinity School in Deerfield, Illinois. He and his wife, Sandy, live in Wildwood, Illinois.

PREFACE

I grew up with Gospel stories. I loved hearing them told over and over. When I entered young adulthood, I decided stories were for children, not for adults. I left them all behind, reading only Jesus's teachings and the epistles, which interpret his stories and teachings. My Christian life limped along in a distortion of what Christianity is meant to be—a distortion that comes to those who ignore Gospel stories.

And then one day I was challenged to read the Gospels—and only the Gospels—for at least a year. I like a challenge, so I embarked on this journey. I had no idea that I would discover that my view of the Christian life was dreadfully distorted. I was shocked to discover how far from true Christlike living I had strayed, and that I needed to radically change my belief and behavior. I am grateful for that challenge and today, although I regularly read other books of the Bible, I never stray very far from the Gospels. They remain my essential reading and a source of perpetual renewal in the Spirit.

Thus, when I found myself unemployed, I embarked on another year of reading and reflecting on the Gospels, thinking I would keep company with the Gospel writers, hoping for support and guidance as I hunted for a job. Instead, I discovered I was keeping company with Jesus himself, and it was in the company of Jesus that I was led through those difficult months of unemployment. Today I look back to that time and know I survived it, endured in faith, because I kept company with Jesus.

This book was born during that long period of unemployment as I struggled to make sense and find meaning for my life without work to give me my identity. I wrote the first drafts of some of these stories then, although only one (from John 21) specifically spoke to me about my struggle with unemployment. This was the story of Peter's encounter with Jesus after the resurrection. I then ignored my rough version of that reflection for years, unable to relive the pain of unemployment. It took courage to go back to that story and rewrite it for this book. I am glad I did. Rewriting it brought healing to my soul.

Indeed, all of the Gospel stories covered in this book relate, in different ways, to my life story, and they have helped me keep company with Jesus in the ups and downs of ordinary life, as well as during extraordinary experiences, such as cancer and unemployment. I can't help but tell my story, intertwining it with the story of Jesus. As a result, I did not choose these particular Gospel stories for the purpose of writing a book; instead, they chose me. As I dared to enter the Gospel stories with my whole being, my life was reflected back to me: I saw myself in each of these stories. As I observed the encounter that took place between Jesus and the person in the actual story, I wondered about my own encounter with Jesus. How *would* I respond? How *should* I respond to reflect true faith?

good beginning

Every Gospel story tells of an encounter with Jesus, the Lord. The responses of the various characters vary greatly in these encounters. Their responses are rarely what we might expect. Some people respond in deep faith, willing to follow Jesus regardless of the cost. Others express no faith at all, no love for Jesus, no qualms about betraying him to his enemies. In some encounters, Jesus seems unreasonable and unjust, and I wonder whether that person ever followed him again. The Gospel writers often fail to record people's responses to Jesus, because the point is to enter the story to encounter Jesus for ourselves and then respond in personal ways. When we do this, we discover that all these stories are about our own lives today.

Yet none of the stories are about us. Each story is about Jesus, his life and ministry on this earth. Through these stories, I come to know him, how he thinks, what he does, how he treats those who encounter him. At times I love him; at others I am bewildered by him. Sometimes I am angry. Frequently, I am awed. In the end I bow in worship. Again and again I discover that each story is also a story of my life. The Gospel stories lead us into a double knowledge—knowing God through knowing our true self, knowing the true self through knowing the Triune God.

However, it is not my life story that I hold up to you. As I studied these stories and saw my life reflected back to me, I realized that my experiences, though personal, were not unique. Other people could identify with what had happened to me and with the insights I had drawn from Gospel stories. By sharing my reflections in this book, perhaps others will be encouraged to bring their own life stories to the Gospels and keep company with Jesus—both on ordinary days and when life throws a few curve balls.

I do not claim to provide a thorough interpretation of these passages; that was never my intention. My primary objective is to hold these stories up, as if a mirror, in order to let you see yourself as the Spirit works within you. I invite you to enter the story of Jesus, taking your own story with you. Examine the details of the passage and discover the power of story to challenge and transform our lives as we seek to keep company with the One who has the power and desire to renew and revive us, Jesus, the Son of God.

I once heard that Isaac Newton claimed if he saw further than anyone else, it was only because he stood on the shoulders of giants. If, in this book, you think that I have seen more than others, it is only because I too have stood on the shoulders of giants: my friends and mentors, too numerous to name, who have kept company with Jesus and with me. They showed me the way, gave me the courage to look further, to reflect more deeply, to disagree with them, to grow through them. I thank them all for the free and friendly space they offered me to develop a more intimate relationship with Jesus, my Lord.

J. L. S.

I. SHE WAS ASKED TO DANCE

Keeping Company with Jesus Brings Freedom to Dance

LUKE 13:10-17

Now [Jesus] was teaching in one of the synagogues on the sabbath. And just then there appeared a woman with a spirit that had crippled her for eighteen years. She was bent over and was quite unable to stand up straight. When Jesus saw her, he called her over and said, "Woman, you are set free from your ailment." When he laid his hands on her, immediately she stood up straight and began praising God. But the leader of the synagogue, indignant because Jesus had cured on the sabbath, kept saying to the crowd, "There are six days on which work ought to be done; come on those days and be cured, and not on the sabbath day." But the Lord answered him and said, "You hypocrites! Does not each of you on the sabbath untie his ox or his donkey from the manger, and lead it away to give it water? And ought not this woman, a daughter of Abraham whom Satan bound for eighteen long years, be set free from this bondage on the sabbath day?" When he said this, all his opponents were put to shame; and the entire crowd was rejoicing at all the wonderful things that he was doing.

People who are bent over and unable to stand up straight cannot dance. The bent-over woman "with a spirit that had crippled her for eighteen years" had not danced for eighteen years. Neither had she stretched in the morning, nor looked up at the stars at night. She had never gone bird watching or hiking, nor probably successfully accomplished the daily tasks of cleaning and cooking for her family. Her condition was plain for all to see. She could not dance, but of course no one had asked her to dance.

I cannot prove it, but I believe after eighteen years she was asked to dance at last. She danced with great joy on the holy Sabbath, in the sacred synagogue, in the presence of—perhaps even in defiance of—the religious leaders. I would like to believe Jesus danced with her in the synagogue, on the Sabbath. Jesus's presence gave her permission—even the boldness of true freedom—to dance the dance that takes us out of ourselves only to bring us back more whole than before; to dance the dance that gives freedom to glide joyfully through life, facing all that it brings rather than running away in fear; to dance the dance we all long for, yet so often resist or even refuse.

Eighteen years is a long time to stand at the edge of life and watch others dance. Waiting in longing, the woman could only hope for her day on the floor. She got there in the end. I believe she danced because I identify with this nameless woman. I too was crippled by an oppressive spirit, and in the end, I too finally heard the invitation to dance and experienced freedom as I stepped out into life.

Unlike this woman, my condition was not plain for all to see—even I remained unaware of my crippled state. I could stretch, look up, bend down, stand up straight, do my daily chores. I could even bird-watch, hike, and bike as much as I desired. It wasn't that I could not dance. I would not dance. I was bound by fears of condemnation and disapproval if I stepped out of line and danced, literally and figuratively, participating in all of life with joy and freedom. For years I ignored those frequent invitations to dance, to enjoy life; I was incapable of believing these gifts came from God. The God I knew through my Christian upbringing was so unlike God revealed in scripture. The God I knew was demanding and never satisfied; I could hear him frequently complaining, "Jackie, you can do better," and condemning, "That's wrong." I could not dare believe God offered joy and freedom because I never experienced this. And so, for a long time I never knew how crippled I was; I never knew I could not dance because I never tried it; I never knew I needed healing because I could not admit imperfection. For too long I failed to understand that those who keep company with Jesus love to dance, as a joyful and grateful expression of their freedom. I feared to dance and refused to try, too ignorant to realize my urgent need for healing.

Luke's nameless woman did know her condition and yet she did not ask for healing. True, she came to the synagogue on the Sabbath where Jesus just happened to be teaching. Was it coincidence? I doubt it. I suspect she had heard stories about Jesus and his amazing compassion and willingness to touch and heal the unclean. Perhaps she went to the synagogue deliberately, hopefully. We do not know because Luke merely states, "and just then there appeared a woman," as though her presence in the synagogue was a surprise. After all, she was considered an unclean person because she lived in an imperfect body, and she was in a very holy place, on a very holy day. Where did she come from and why was she there?

It is easy for us today to assume that she came because Jesus, the healer, was the guest teacher that day. Healers usually attract crowds of needy people. It seems logical that in those days of Jesus's earthly ministry, if you needed healing, you would seek him out. Did she go for healing that day? I am not sure we can assume that she did.

First, she was a Jew, and therefore familiar with the law that interpreted healing as work, thus prohibited on the Sabbath. It is hard for us to imagine a religion that taught God would rather let a person suffer and even die than to be healed on the Sabbath. I want to believe that today I live in a more enlightened and compassionate time. Then I remember how driven I have been about getting to church on time each Sunday, even when it meant neglecting to show compassion to someone in need. I feared what others would think of me if I skipped church to pray with a suffering neighbor. Or what their reaction might be if I came into to church late, dirty, and disheveled because I paused to help a homeless person who happened to cross my path. Sadly, I have ignored opportunities to heal. I have been too concerned about keeping up appearances at church. And I wonder whether this attitude discouraged others from seeking help from Jesus in the church.

Back to the question. A second reason the woman probably did not expect healing is because, with her imperfect body, she was not welcome in the synagogue on any day of the week, let alone the Sabbath. She did not expect to be welcomed on this day, and so she crept in unnoticed and hidden in the crowd. She also would not, indeed could not, speak up and request healing—not in the synagogue. Women had to remain silent. Only men could talk out loud and pray. The crippled woman did not dare come forward on her own initiative. She could only hope that Jesus would notice her. She could only hope that Jesus's behavior would be different from all her past experiences with religious leaders and that he would be willing to offer healing. She could only pray silently, "To dance at last, and in your company, O merciful Lord."

There were stories about this healer and rabbi that the woman had no doubt heard, stories of how he had defied the religious leaders once before, even healing on the Sabbath and in the synagogue (Luke 6:6-11). On that occasion the scribes and Pharisees were the first to observe the man with his infirmity—a withered hand. The religious leaders had even hoped Jesus would heal him so "they might find an accusation against him." Jesus courageously ignored them then. He called the man forward and publicly healed him. The scribes and Pharisees who saw the miracle "were filled with fury" and immediately began discussing ways to get rid of Jesus.

If the woman knew about this healing, it would hardly have encouraged her. After all she was a woman with a more severe infirmity. The man had only a withered hand compared to her crippled body. She would not have dared hope Jesus would again defy the religious leaders, again incur their wrath, again risk his life for another. She did not know that Jesus came precisely for this—to sacrifice his life for her life and also our lives. And so she remained unseen and silent in that crowded synagogue where Jesus was teaching. She watched and listened and imagined the joy of healing and dancing.

Jesus refused to be dominated by a religion that failed to show mercy. As always, his actions got him into trouble with religious leaders, these so-called holy men, who remained strangers to the holiness they promoted, strangers to the dancing they banned. They were an oppressive group who burdened people with their rigid and biased interpretations of God's word. Their numerous additions to God's law enslaved rather than liberated. It is not surprising that Jesus, on one occasion, condemned the religious leaders, saying of them, "They tie up heavy burdens, hard to bear, and lay them on the shoulders of others; but they themselves are unwilling to lift a finger to move them" (Matthew 23:4).

The religious leaders hated Jesus, hated being in his company, because they loved their own interpretations of the law too much. Jesus consistently defied them, reaching out to all those who had been crippled by heavy burdens laid on their shoulders by religious leaders, teaching them to dance at last. I wonder what Jesus was preaching about on this Sabbath day. The topic is not mentioned, but I do know that he was not teaching just to impress others with his amazing communication skills and understanding of scripture. He never cared about the opinions of others; he only cared about his Father's opinion. Jesus taught because he had compassion for people. Mark informs us that after an exhausting day of teaching the demanding crowd and healing their sick, Jesus went across the Sea of Galilee for solitude and rest. The crowd followed him, thinking nothing of interrupting his prayerful solitude. Seeing them, Jesus "had compassion for them, because they were like sheep without a shepherd; and he began to teach them many things" (Mark 6:34).[1] His teaching was compassionate because it freed rather than enslaved, brought healing and life rather than sickness and death, offered grace and mercy rather than condemnation and judgment, dancing rather than rigidity, the presence of God rather than the absence of God.

Because Jesus taught with compassion, he always stopped and attended to a person in need, regardless of all the wonderful truths he had planned to share. On this Sabbath, Jesus immediately stopped teaching when he saw the woman unable to stand up straight. Not even an uncaring crowd could keep her hidden from his caring eyes. Not even his enemies, who were searching for the least infringement on their interpretation of scripture, could discourage Jesus's compassion. I often wonder how Jesus spotted her in that crowded synagogue. What attracted his attention so that he looked directly at the crippled woman, seeing her urgent need for healing? She surely wasn't the only needy person longing for healing in that crowded synagogue. Yet Jesus looked past them all, his heart going out to this one woman who had not danced for eighteen years.

We might think that compassion for this crippled woman is not really remarkable. After all, any human is bound to feel compassion for a woman permanently bent over. Her condition deserved it. And yet Jesus's compassion is remarkable. He took a risk. It cost him his reputation. The gatekeepers of Israel's religion were there, watching and waiting. They were adamant about abstaining from anything that even seemed like work on the Sabbath, and they longed to condemn Jesus once and for all. Jesus's compassion is also remarkable because Jesus healed and freed a woman, and then did nothing to stop her burst of praise in the male-controlled synagogue.

To Jesus, it did not matter that she was a woman. Neither did it matter that he was in the synagogue as a guest teacher that Sabbath. Jesus was not afraid to break through all traditions and laws for the sake of compassion. He taught in accordance with his Father and thus challenged judgmental Pharisees with the demand, "Go and learn what this means, 'I desire mercy, not sacrifice'" (Matthew 9:13).[2] The woman could not hide from his merciful eyes, could not escape the invitation to dance, which rang loudly through the synagogue that morning. Jesus, as Luke simply puts it, "called her over." Presumably he called her up front where everyone in that crowded synagogue could see her. This was no secret healing.

She made a slow and painful journey to the front of the synagogue, where Jesus waited patiently and lovingly, ready to pronounce the healing words: "Woman, you are set free from your ailment." Not merely healed, but freed. Freed from an oppressive spirit that had crippled her for far too long. Freed to dance at last as the Healer laid his compassionate hands on her. In response, Luke records, "Immediately she stood up straight and began praising God." Nothing would stop this woman's praise. Did she also take Jesus's hand and invite him to dance with her? I hope so. I think he would have liked that.

It could not have been easy for this woman to accept Jesus's invitation to come forward. For her, walking was slow and difficult, perhaps even painful; certainly it was agonizing to watch. Jesus had the power to heal her from a distance. He once healed a royal official's son in Capernaum while himself remaining in Cana, a distance of about eighteen miles (John 4:46-54). He surely could have healed the women in her pew and saved her the embarrassing walk to the front. But he did not do that. The woman had to go through more suffering before being healed. Why?

I believe Jesus always had reasons for what he did, although reasons are rarely stated by the Gospel writers or are hidden in the text. Therefore I keep pondering. When I discover a reason for this particular story, it will teach me as much about myself as the story. As many great saints have insisted, knowledge of self is essential to knowledge of God. In other words, keeping company with Jesus will mean getting to know myself. And so I meditate on Jesus's possible reasons, on the lesson for the religious leaders, for the woman herself, for the crowds in the synagogue and, of course, for every Christian since that day. I cannot jump too quickly to the story's application to my life today. I have to begin first with the story of Jesus and this woman in need of healing.

I think the lesson for the religious leaders is obvious. They were opposed to Jesus and against working on the Sabbath. They misinterpreted the Mosaic Law and consequently enslaved their congregations rather than freeing them. Their picture of God was a gross distortion of the picture revealed in Scripture. In deliberately confronting the religious leaders' views about the Sabbath, Jesus was giving a true picture of God. Jesus's actions proclaimed that God heals and frees the needy, regardless of gender, age, or day of the week. This was one of the main reasons the religious leaders hated Jesus. He showed them up as false interpreters and incompetent gatekeepers of God's holy law.

The lesson for the crowd relates to this lesson for the religious leaders. When the woman began her dance of grateful joy, "the entire crowd was rejoicing at all the wonderful things [Jesus] was doing." I imagine them all dancing in their pews and down the aisles. And then I wonder why were they *all* rejoicing? Jesus had healed a nameless and unknown woman. What had she done to deserve this spontaneous praise at her healing? There is no record of an eruption of praise when Jesus miraculously fed more than five thousand hungry men, women, and children.[3] But here one unknown woman is healed and the synagogue is in a joyous uproar. Perhaps the praise was not so much because healing had taken place; rather, it might have been because Jesus had once again defied their oppressive leaders by healing and freeing on the Sabbath, thus reiterating the truth that he came to give life, and to give it abundantly (John 10:10). The oppressed crowd would have been assured of the freedom that comes to those who keep company with Jesus. They would have witnessed that nothing—not even powerful religious leaders—could take this freedom away from them. They would have recognized that in healing and freeing the woman, Jesus was able to heal and free them all. This could have been the lesson they gladly took from this event and the reason they erupted in joyful praise, rejoicing with this unknown woman.

As a member of a congregation, I see lessons for myself. In the Western world, we live in an individualistic culture and tend to privatize our relationships with Jesus. We forget that being in Jesus's company also means being in company with his friends: we belong to each other as members of the body of

Christ (Romans 12:5). Our relationship with Jesus, although intensely personal, is also public. The woman's healing was public; she was not healed from a distance and in secret.

There is more. Our Western culture tends to believe that all suffering is bad and ought to be avoided whenever possible. We even expect Jesus to smooth our path and make life easier for us. When I lost my job, I was convinced I would quickly be employed again, with a minimum of pain and inconvenience. Jesus, I naively assumed, would not make me suffer through endless months of waiting. But he did, and I nearly gave up on my Christian faith. My picture of Jesus and the Christian life was grossly distorted.

This story confronts my distortions. There could be no healing for this woman so long as she remained in the comfort of her private pew, hidden in the crowd. She had to act, even though it cost her. The story shatters my illusion that Jesus's compassion will ensure I avoid pain and suffering and sorrow, that he will rush in to protect me and never ask me to do anything that might hurt. There are times when Jesus will ask each of us to follow a difficult path. And we will learn, as others have learned before us, that there is no joy without sorrow, no gain without pain. Those who truly desire healing, even spiritual healing, will often have to make this difficult, time-consuming, obedient step of faith toward Jesus. We have the responsibility to respond to Jesus's invitation, despite the cost to ourselves.

Let me return to the story. In response to her healing, the woman rejoiced and the crowd joined in. But the synagogue leader became agitated; there was no praise from him, no joy at the healing and freedom of a woman after eighteen years of enslavement. According to Luke, the synagogue leader was indignant, believing Jesus had profaned the synagogue by healing on the Sabbath. He was angry with Jesus, but he lacked the courage to confront Jesus himself. Instead, he took it out on the people. He turned to the congregation and vented his resentment. "There are six days on which work ought to be done," he said. "Come on those days and be cured, and not on the sabbath day." According to Luke, he kept saying it; perhaps this was because the rejoicing of the people was so loud no one heard him. The people praised; their ruler complained. The people stomped their feet in rejoicing; he stamped his feet in anger. He could not praise, and I bet he could not dance.

And yet I think I can understand this leader and sympathize with him, albeit just a little. He had a job to do and wanted to do it correctly. Perhaps he was driven by the need to be perfect. I know I have been. Like this ruler, I was sure I knew the law of God and was committed to obeying it perfectly. I was driven to keep the rules even if it meant neglecting to show compassion to another in need. Too often I have sat down in resentment over a perceived hurt, while others joyfully danced around me. The best we can say of the ruler is that he had backbone because he stood up for what he believed to be right. But he was not a free and whole man; rather, he made obedience to the rules his sole concern, and ignored the real needs of people. I suspect that he studied his Scriptures and examined his theology in isolation, and so failed to see how devastatingly cruel the effects of his legalistic perfectionism were, failed to see that it not only crippled him but also his congregation. Gradually the law became more important to him than the people. His heart became hard, and he was reluctant to let the people dance because he would not dance himself.

If the leader lacked the courage to confront Jesus himself, Jesus had the courage and compassion to confront not only this man but also all oppressive religious leaders. "You hypocrites," the Son of Man accused, as he reminded them that they showed more compassion for their thirsty beasts than for this woman. He dared to elevate her status, proclaiming her "a daughter of Abraham," one of them, one with them, belonging to God, gender notwithstanding.

If I think that I understand the synagogue leader, I know I understand the crippled woman. Her story is my story. True, I was never bent over double. I have always been able to stretch in the morning and look up at the stars at night. Yet although I could, I never would dance, because I was just as bound by legalism as the synagogue ruler.

Sometimes I wonder whether religion of the day, with all its rules and heavy burdens, was the spirit that crippled this woman. I know it was that strict religious viewpoint that once crippled me. I grew up with a religion that preached grace but practiced law, that turned holiness into rules, an endless list of dos and don'ts—mostly don'ts. Recognition, approval, even forgiveness were based on my religious observances. I became meekly submissive to rules, even adding rules of my own just to impress. Near the top of the list was, "Don't dance." I never did, never dared to provoke disapproval from leaders I thought mattered. I did not dance literally or figuratively and neither did I live in the fullness of joy Jesus promised to all who live in his company (John 15:11). I failed to understand that Jesus's company brings liberty, not oppression. Because I feared this freedom, I also feared keeping company with Jesus.

Crippled for years by prohibitions, legalism, and injustices, I could not dance—not even when I desperately wanted to. And yet I never asked for healing. I did not know I needed it. The woman in Luke's story did not ask because she was not sure Jesus would work on the Sabbath in the synagogue. Jesus offered her healing anyway. And when he did, she came forward as quickly as her crippled body allowed.

It took me a long time, but I finally heard Jesus's offer of healing, heard his invitation to the dance. A number of experiences helped me to grow into the freedom of living in Jesus's presence. In my early thirties, I was preparing to lead a Bible study on Hebrews 10. Something I read in that chapter, I no longer know what, suddenly made me realize that God hates legalism and its inevitable hypocrisy. Had I only paid attention to Jesus in the Gospels, I would have known this. I heard God lovingly say to me, "Jackie, give up your list of rules." I quickly responded, "I can't. You know my rules keep me a good Christian." I failed to see the hypocrisy in that sentence. Again God challenged, "Jackie, give up your list." I continued to argue while God patiently waited for me to get the point. Finally I fearfully gave up my list, bowing in humble submission before God. I wondered how I was going to live the Christian life without my list. I returned to Hebrews and read the answer: "My righteous one will live by faith" (10:38). That day, I began the journey to the dance floor, although I still was not ready or able to dance.

A year or so later, a second experience got me onto the floor, even dancing. I had just begun my teaching career at a college in Johannesburg. My first few months had not been easy, and I was struggling and even becoming angry with God. One Sunday evening I sat in church listening to a sermon on "six steps to backsliding," based on the life of David. The preacher turned David's story into a series of behaviors to avoid and principles to live by. His message took me back into that legalism God had challenged me to give up. There in my church pew, I angrily and silently muttered to God, "If this is what Christianity is all about, I quit now!" Once again, I heard God's loving voice, "Let's talk about it," I responded with, "You bet we will talk about this."

I never did talk about it. On my way home from church I suddenly realized that I had a relationship with the Almighty God, one that lovingly desired my presence despite my anger and temper tantrums. I remembered the story in John's Gospel, the day many superficial followers of Jesus turned away. Jesus turned to the few who remained and asked, "Do you also wish to go away?" I identified with Peter's response: "Lord, to whom can we go? You have the words of eternal life" (John 6:67-68). That was the day I finally began to dance. My Christian life now focused on a loving relationship with God in Christ Jesus rather than on my need to follow rules to the letter to impress others.

I heard God's invitation to dance, and like the crippled woman, I made my slow and painful move closer and closer to where Jesus stood and waited for me. When I finally got there, I found my feet. I stood up straight, praised God for unbounded freedom, and began to dance. That is why I believe the woman in Luke's Gospel danced—and even asked Jesus to join her.

Like this woman, I also discovered a community of fellow companions of Jesus who love to dance with me. I am dancing, at last, in good company, the company of Jesus and his friends.

❖ ❖ ❖

Questions for Reflection or Discussion

1. In what ways do the practices of Christianity "cripple" (emotionally and perhaps even physically) people today? What do you think we could do to avoid oppressive religious/church structures?

2. The synagogue leader was indignant because Jesus healed on the Sabbath. Do you see possible similarities in the church today, where a Christian leader or layperson is more concerned with adherence to rules and regulations than showing mercy? How can we seek to change this in our own lives and church?

3. Who are "the crippled with a spirit" in your church, community, and world? How can the church free them to dance with joy?

2. "NEITHER DO I CONDEMN YOU"

Keeping Company with Jesus Even When I Have Sinned

JOHN 8:1-11

Then each of them went home, while Jesus went to the Mount of Olives. Early in the morning he came again to the temple. All the people came to him and he sat down and began to teach them. The scribes and the Pharisees brought a woman who had been caught in adultery; and making her stand before all of them, they said to him, "Teacher, this woman was caught in the very act of committing adultery. Now in the law Moses commanded us to stone such women. Now what do you say?" They said this to test him, so that they might have some charge to bring against him. Jesus bent down and wrote with his finger on the ground. When they kept on questioning him, he straightened up and said to them, "Let anyone among you who is without sin be the first to throw a stone at her." And once again he bent down and wrote on the ground. When they heard it, they went away, one by one, beginning with the elders; and Jesus was left alone with the woman standing before him. Jesus straightened up and said to her, "Woman, where are they? Has no one condemned you?" She said, "No one, sir." And Jesus said, "Neither do I condemn you. Go your way, and from now on do not sin again."

"Jesus bent down and wrote with his finger on the ground."
The detail in this sentence is remarkable yet unnecessary.
How else can a person write with his or her finger on the
ground unless they bend down, even if sitting? A writer who
pays this much attention to detail should be expected to
"tell all," but the writer of this passage fails to do that. Having told us so much, arousing our curiosity and interest, the
writer leaves us guessing about what Jesus wrote with his
finger on the ground that early morning. This question has
fascinated Bible readers, teachers, and preachers for centuries. I too am intrigued and wonder about what the
Gospel did not record. What did Jesus write when he bent
down that day long ago?

There is another mystery to this story. Although this
account appears in John's Gospel, it was most likely written
after the completion of this Gospel. The story is not found in
the most reliable ancient Greek manuscripts to which we
have access. As New Testament scholar Alan Culpepper
notes, "It appears to be an early, free-flowing unit of tradition that did not find a secure home in the written Gospels."[1]
It is certainly an interpolation in John's Gospel, breaking the
continuity of a narrative that begins in 7:52 and resumes in
8:12. "Nevertheless," writes John Sanford in his commentary
on John's Gospel, "the story is part of valid Christian tradition and was included in John's Gospel by people who had
their reasons for feeling it belonged."[2] Fortunately, someone
recognized the value of this event and preserved it for us.
There is no doubt in my mind that the story is genuine,
reflecting the character of Jesus, who shows mercy to sinners, even unrepentant sinners, and condemns hypocrisy,
sometimes angrily, always compassionately. I want to keep
company with this Jesus.

It is possible that whoever recorded this event was
both a good and courageous storyteller, able to trust the

process of storytelling, and therefore he deliberately left out the intriguing detail of Jesus's message in the sand. A good story presents without describing, shows rather than tells. As pastor and author Eugene Peterson notes, "Stories invite us into a world other than ourselves, and, if they are good and true stories, a world larger than ourselves. Bible stories are good and true stories, and the world they invite us into is the world of God's creation and salvation and blessing."[3] It is the responsibility of the reader to prayerfully reflect on the story, thinking with the mind in the heart, paying attention with every faculty, taking in every detail, discovering newness even in a well-known story. The reader of Gospel stories should remain open, willingly submitting to the Spirit of God to use the story for ongoing "creation and salvation and blessing," being made free to live in Jesus's company.

Maybe the writer of John was a good storyteller and omitted this detail to pique our interest. On the other hand, perhaps the writer simply did not know what Jesus wrote with his finger on the ground. Perhaps no one could tell him. Jesus's words were never revealed to those who were present and observed this event and were, therefore, always unknown. Either way, it will always remain a mystery to us, inviting us to use our imaginations and to wonder. I speculate about this incident because I believe the words were significant. I invite you to imagine with me and then decide for yourself.

Let me set the story in context as the writer does. He begins with the information that, the night before, "each of them went home, while Jesus went to the Mount of Olives." Yet again our writer has said at once too much and too little. Who were "each of them" who went home that night? Since the story is an interpolation in the text, we do not know for sure. We can only assume, since the writer maintains that

Jesus "came again to the temple" the next morning, that it was the crowd, the religious leaders, and others in the temple the day before who went home.

The point the writer is making is that Jesus went to the mountain alone that night. Why would the writer highlight this unexplained fact? It is likely that the first readers of this story understood the significance of being alone on a mountain and needed no explanation. The mountain was a symbol of God's presence and meant something specific to those familiar with Hebrew Scripture. Going to a mountain was understood as going to be in the presence of God. People went to mountains to pray. Thus we can safely assume Jesus went there to pray on the night before a woman caught in adultery was brought into his company.

At daybreak Jesus returned to the temple in Jerusalem, "where all the people gathered around him" (John 8:2 NIV). The people were up early that morning, not wanting to miss anything Jesus said or did. As was customary for teachers in those days, Jesus sat down before he began to teach. Almost immediately, he was rudely interrupted by the scribes and Pharisees, those religious leaders whom everyone respected as holy and close to God. They were the men the community looked to for guidance in the spiritual life. Usually people paid attention when they spoke. And usually the religious leaders made holiness so impossible the people did not even try to attain it, believing they could never achieve it.

On this occasion, the crowd paid attention because the leaders brought along "Exhibit A." Forcefully and with authority, they came through the crowd with what I can only assume was a reluctant woman. I can almost hear their arrogant demands as they made their way to Jesus. "Make way, make way," they would have cried aloud. "Do not touch, do not touch. This woman is unclean and will make you all unclean." The crowd quickly stepped aside, curious to see what the leaders intended. Finally, in great triumph the group arrived up front, where Jesus sat silently waiting. There was no teaching during this loud and ungracious interruption. "Making her stand before all of them," they put the woman on public display. They wanted her to be seen, her protests notwithstanding. I imagine she protested the injustice of the treatment she was receiving. Who wouldn't? She was forced against her will to be there, treated like a trapped criminal. Then, in what I imagine was a loud, pompous, perhaps even rehearsed unison, they complained, "Teacher, this woman was caught in the very act of committing adultery." And they proceeded to enlighten Jesus to the law of Moses concerning those caught in adultery, as if Jesus did not know. These arrogant religious leaders failed to realize that their condemnation of the woman was an even greater condemnation of themselves.

A number of details fascinate me. First, the scribes and Pharisees: the writer has included the detail that this all happened "early in the morning." I wonder how the scribes and Pharisees knew where and when to go, in order to catch this woman in the "very act of committing adultery"? After all, adultery is a private and secretive act. No one knows ahead of time where someone can be caught committing adultery, unless the couple is reported or the adultery is a set-up.

A second detail that fascinates me is the information about being caught "in the very act of committing adultery." Her accusers proudly announced this detail to Jesus and the listening curious crowd. Yet adultery requires two people. This can only mean that the man was still with her when these so-called "holy" men barged in and arrested her. Why was only the woman brought before Jesus and accused of sin? Where was the man who had been lying with her? Did he perhaps use the old line, the one that began with Adam, that sounds something like, "The woman you gave me, she made me do it."[4] And was this seen as a good enough excuse? Or was the man excused because he was used to set the woman up? Perhaps the man was one of them, a fellow scribe or Pharisee, sent purposefully to entrap a poor woman—maybe a prostitute, which was often the only way for a poor, single woman in that time to make a living and stay alive.

Her partner was as guilty as she, yet only the woman was condemned and forced to stand before Jesus. The Mosaic Law demanded not only the death of the adulterous woman but also the adulterous man (Leviticus 20:10; Deuteronomy 22:23-24). Did these accusers conveniently or deliberately forget that when they pompously rehearsed the law for Jesus? Perhaps, if this was a setup.

I might be willing to excuse the religious leaders if their desire was for the salvation of this poor woman. But to my amazement, these keepers of Israel's religion, these ministers of the grace of God, did not bring the woman to Jesus out of compassionate concern for a sinner needing God's grace. Their intent was not her repentance, healing, and transformation but rather their own aggrandizement and justification. By accusing this woman they hoped to look more holy before the people. And more to the point, they desired to make Jesus look more foolish to the crowd. Their accusation was intended, the storyteller claims, "to test [Jesus], so that they might have some charge to bring against him." They were looking for an excuse to do away with Jesus and regain their authority over the crowds. The woman was a mere pawn in their evil game, which further leads me to believe this was a setup.

In their minds the test was very simple. The Mosaic Law demanded that adulterers be put to death by stoning. Yet at that time, Israel was under occupation by the Romans and subject to Roman law. Jews were not free to enforce their laws; neither were they free to condemn another to death by stoning. Had Jesus responded by demanding immediate stone-throwing in obedience to Mosaic Law, he could have been accused of insurrection against the governing Romans. But had he suggested submitting to Roman law, he could have been accused of undermining Mosaic Law, and therefore of being against God. Either way, the leaders were convinced they had finally trapped Jesus.

I suspect the scribes and Pharisees eagerly waited to pounce on Jesus the minute he spoke, with their accusation, "You see, we warned you this man was not from God. He deserves to die." They failed to consider that there might be a response other than what they had envisioned. They showed no compassion for a sinner caught in the act of breaking God's law. It is no wonder Jesus bent down to write with his finger on the ground, refusing to either look at or respond to them.

Meanwhile, the crowd silently watched and waited. They too invite our reflection. What were they thinking? Did the religious leaders impress or disgust them? If any members of the crowd were aware of the injustice perpetrated against this woman, they failed to protest. No one asked where the male adulterer was. It makes me wonder if it was more typical for women to be accused and punished at that time. Had people become so immune to this type of injustice that no one thought it peculiar that the man was not accused of wrongdoing? Was it commonly held that men must be submitted to, even when the men were wrong? Whatever their thoughts, the crowd remained silent as they waited to see how Jesus would respond, how he would extricate himself from this trap.

I put myself in that crowd, feeling the growing tension as they waited for Jesus to make his judgment. Ignoring them all, Jesus continued silently writing on the ground. I marvel at his courage to let undisturbed silence rule for so long, to pay no heed to the noisy and demanding accusers. But then Jesus was a teacher of great courage; he refused to give demanding people what they expected and wanted. He gave only what was needed. He was sufficiently secure in himself as a person and teacher that his listeners' conclusions did not influence him unduly.

Jesus was not afraid to use silence as a teaching tool, a tool that provides inevitable space for individual self-reflection. If they thought his silence indicated ignorance or fear of reprisal, so be it. He was willing to take that risk and experience the inevitable tension and embarrassment of the people. They expected authoritative words. Jesus gave them silence. He did not change his approach to please the people. I believe that in the silence, he patiently hoped the accusers would examine their own lives and confess their own sins before daring to condemn an oppressed woman, one they had possibly set up in the first place.

Yet I am not sure anyone in the story took advantage of Jesus's grace and patience to examine his or her own life. They were all too intent on waiting to see what Jesus would say and do. They waited in vain. Calmly ignoring them all, he bent down and wrote with his finger on the ground. Feet shuffled, people looked around, whispered conversations took place between groups. The atmosphere grew ever more tense, and the people ever more nervous. Silence is too revealing to be endured without discomfort. As I, in my imagination, look around the crowd, I see myself in the different people, thinking different thoughts, remaining for different reasons, despite the growing discomfort of Jesus's silence. Enter the story and imagine with me.

Within the crowd there were surely a number of sinners, those who knew their willful wrongdoing but were too overwhelmed or discouraged to seek repentance. The sin would vary, but perhaps there were other adulterers, maybe even the man who was with the adulterous woman that morning. They were all anxious to hear what Jesus would say. If he sided with the leaders, they too would be doomed, condemned to a life beyond the grace of God. It was a tense moment for them. They could only hope for mercy.

I am sure there were also other legalists in the crowd besides the scribes and Pharisees. These are the people who are convinced that the law is clear and obedience is a simple matter. Legalists are more concerned with strict adherence to the letter of the law than compassion for sinners caught in sinful behavior. Legalists often believe that we ought not to be compassionate to unrepentant sinners, that compassion is tantamount to endorsement of the sin. The legalists in the story waited for Jesus to bring down the law in all its force, and they probably wondered why he took so long to respond. Legalists are uncomfortable in the company of Jesus.

Although the story makes no mention of them, we can presume that Jesus's disciples were also there that morning. As far as we know, this event took place during the last week of Jesus's life and his disciples stayed with him as much as possible. They had left their families, given up all they owned to follow Jesus. If he could not extricate himself from this clever trap, they too would go down. Did they wonder, "He doesn't seem to know what to do. Have I made a mistake to forsake all and follow him?"

And, of course, the woman caught in the act waited. One word from Jesus and her life could be ended or transformed for good. Her fate was now totally in his hands.

The crowd, the disciples, and the woman waited in uncomfortable, anxious silence. Not so the religious leaders. If they were disturbed by Jesus's silent response, they were not themselves silenced. They failed to take advantage of the grace Jesus's silence gave them. They remained blindly assured of their own righteousness, neither discerning sin in their own lives nor withdrawing their accusation and apologizing to the woman. The writer states that, "they kept on questioning him" until Jesus reluctantly sat up and commanded, "Let anyone among you who is without sin be the first to throw a stone at her."

Up to that point in the story, I suspect people assumed only the woman was guilty of sin—after all, only she had been brought to Jesus and accused. It is an insidious belief, even among many Christians today, that as long as we don't get caught, we are not guilty of wrongdoing. We hold onto our belief until we hear Jesus command, "Whoever is sinless, cast the first stone." His command levels the playing field. No one was better than the woman. Not the scribes and Pharisees who made the accusation; not the disciples who faithfully followed Jesus; not a single person in the waiting crowd. No one was guiltless. Jesus's response meant that everyone, including Jesus's disciples, had to examine themselves rather than the woman, to see their own sin and not just hers. She was guilty; so were they.

So "one by one, beginning with the elders," the people slipped away in guilty silence, even Jesus's disciples. No one was comfortable in his presence any longer. No one dared remain. It was not long before "Jesus was left alone with the woman standing before him." This detail is remarkable. The publicly condemned sinner did not leave! I marvel at this aspect of the story. She could have left. After giving his command, Jesus did not watch to see what happened. He again bent down to write on the ground. The woman had her chance to break away, but she chose to remain.

The woman's behavior intrigues me the most. I am not good at handling myself when I have been caught in wrongdoing. I am ashamed and want to hide as quickly as possible. And I have been caught only by fellow sinners! No one has ever publicly dragged me before the sinless Son of God. I think I might have been the first to slip away that morning. What was it like to be this woman, to stand before Jesus with her sin publicly exposed? And, when she had the opportunity to slip away, why didn't she take it? What kept her there, alone, after everyone else had left? Did it have something to do with what Jesus wrote on the ground, what the writer failed to reveal to us? If so, the words Jesus wrote were highly significant and we do well to wonder about it.

For a while I considered whether Jesus was merely doodling out of embarrassment. This is probably how I would have reacted in a similar circumstance. The behavior of the spiritual leaders—his religious male peers—was terrible, and their treatment of the woman was unloving and cruel. Perhaps Jesus was ashamed for them. But the longer I reflected, I could not imagine an embarrassed person having the courage to remain silent before a crowd that anxiously waited for his response. I know I could not.

I am not the only one to ponder this mystery. For centuries, Bible readers have speculated about what Jesus wrote. There are some later manuscripts of John's Gospel that even have words added to the story that suggest Jesus wrote down the sins of each of those present. Other scholars wonder whether Jesus did not write the names of other women with whom the judgmental scribes and Pharisees had committed adultery. After all, we often condemn the very sin we most struggle with ourselves. Other people have suggested that perhaps Jesus wrote out the Ten Commandments or verses from Exodus 23 about avoiding false witness and lies.[5]

All of these suggestions relate to the scribes and Pharisees, the assumption being that Jesus wrote a message designed for them alone. But would they have been able to see what Jesus wrote on the ground, and if they had, wouldn't they have been silenced, perhaps even slipped away quickly and quietly before Jesus spoke? If the message was for them, why did Jesus bend down again and write even as they were all leaving his company? They would have never seen his message.

I discarded all these theories and speculations and began reflecting on a very different question: *For whom did Jesus write?* If Jesus's writing was significant (I believe it was), if it was not mere doodling (I believe it wasn't), then he wrote it for a specific, even limited audience. Only those closest to him that morning would have seen what he wrote. This means that Jesus wrote a message intended for the eyes of a specific person or persons. The question is, who?

This is yet another problem the writer fails to solve for us. And so I imagine the scene once again. I see the teacher bending down to write on the ground, thus avoiding eye contact with everyone there. I see a silent group of people impatiently waiting for his answer.

Let's imagine I am the teacher. If I want people to see what I am writing, I would not bend down and write on the ground. My very "bendedness" would immediately obscure my words from most people. If I want the whole crowd of people to see, I would write my message on a board or use modern technology like PowerPoint to ensure the whole group has a good view. I would not bend down and neither would I write on the ground, unless I want only a limited audience to see what I write. Based on this, I believe that Jesus's message was not intended for the whole crowd.

It is also unlikely the woman's accusers were close enough to see. They were impatiently waiting to pronounce Jesus a fraud. Any message for them would surely have silenced them, not kept them persisting in judgment against the woman. If he was writing down names of their adulterous partners, I am sure they would have been instantly silenced, even have slipped away in embarrassment. It seems unlikely that Jesus wrote a message for the scribes and Pharisees in the sand that morning.

Neither do I think the disciples were close enough to see what Jesus wrote. If they had been, surely they would have remembered it and passed it on to those who wrote down the Gospel story. They did not. So we can assume that the message was not for them.

That leaves only one possibility—the woman. The message was for her eyes only. The writer makes the point of stating that she alone was left standing before Jesus. Only the woman caught in adultery would have seen this message that Jesus continued writing even as everyone deserted. Would it then have been a message of love and compassion, of grace and forgiveness, of respect and justice? Did Jesus assure her of all this despite her lifestyle of sin? Is that why she chose to remain in Jesus's presence when everyone else left him, to read again and again a message that brought life to her soul? Did she stay to keep on receiving grace and mercy freely offered by the sinless Savior? Whatever her reasons, she stayed and thus she, and she alone, heard those words of healing forgiveness and transformation spoken by the Savior.

Some years ago a student (I'll call her Mayvis) sat down at my desk, looked me in the eye, and announced, "You know my story, don't you?" Of course I did not, but I waited patiently in silence. I knew she would give me clues. "The lesson today gave me away," she said. I reflected back to class. We had studied this story. I remembered that Mayvis looked at me with undivided attention, hardly daring to breath. "That Gospel woman's story is your story," I correctly guessed. Mayvis went on to tell me of her struggle to overcome her habits of sexual promiscuity. Judgmental church leaders with their merciless condemnation had only entrenched her in destructive patterns. Not until she finally changed churches and met church leaders who offered her grace—not condemnation—and space for healing—not judgmental accusations—was she able to change. This story was truly her story. I wonder today what message she would imagine Jesus wrote for her.

I am glad the writer failed to record what Jesus wrote. If the message was for that woman only, it would have been very personal and thus irrelevant to you and me today. But I can now imagine a message that Jesus would write to me, a sinner, a message that would keep me close to the compassionate, sinless Son of God—a message that would encourage me to remain in his company, to keep on receiving grace and mercy. Perhaps you too can imagine a message that Jesus would have just for you, and no one else, that is appropriate for your sin, and no one else's, that might keep you in his company even though everyone else guiltily slips away. And, just as he said to the adulterous woman then, so too he says to you and me today: "Neither do I condemn you. Go your way, and from now on do not sin again."

QUESTIONS FOR REFLECTION OR DISCUSSION

1. Only John recorded this story. Since John specifically stated his purpose as "that you may believe Jesus in the Christ the Son of God" (John 20:31), how do you think this story helps affirm our faith in Jesus?

2. For what possible reasons, in your opinion, did Jesus respond to the religious leaders with total silence? What was he hoping they would do? Why does it take courage for a teacher to let silence rule? Why do you think this is important?

3. Prayerfully reflect on possible words Jesus would write "for your eyes only." What words would keep you in his presence when everyone else disappears? Share these words with others as you feel comfortable.

3. "The Other Nine, Where Are They?"

Keeping Company with Jesus Cultivates Gratitude

Luke 17:11-19

On the way to Jerusalem Jesus was going through the region between Samaria and Galilee. As he entered a village, ten lepers approached him. Keeping their distance, they called out, saying, "Jesus, Master, have mercy on us!" When he saw them, he said to them, "Go and show yourselves to the priests." And as they went, they were made clean. Then one of them, when he saw that he was healed, turned back, praising God with a loud voice. He prostrated himself at Jesus's feet and thanked him. And he was a Samaritan. Then Jesus asked, "Were not ten made clean? But the other nine, where are they? Was none of them found to return and give praise to God except this foreigner?" Then he said to him, "Get up and go on your way; your faith has made you well."

I believe in gratitude. I enjoy being around grateful people, and when possible, I try to avoid ungrateful people. One summer I worked at a camp for disabled children. I loved helping the ones who were grateful, appreciative of every little thing I did for them. I did not mind helping them even when the task was messy and dirty, involving sacrifice on my part. The thankfulness of those I helped made it easy. I would have avoided the ungrateful children if that were possible. Gratitude, I learned, is truly a worthy virtue.

I also believe gratitude is an essential Christian virtue, perhaps even a mark of true Christianity. It is evidenced in those who keep company with Jesus. To give thanks to the Lord for all things, at all times, and in all circumstances is one of those difficult commands Paul urged on Christians in Ephesus and Thessalonica in Asia Minor (Ephesians 5:20; 1 Thessalonians 5:18). Although Jesus himself never actually demanded gratitude, at least once he expressed disappointed surprise at the lack of gratitude after a miraculous healing. That was the day he healed ten lepers. Only one came back to express gratitude. Jesus was amazed, the Gospel maintains, perhaps even upset at this. He wondered, "Were not ten made clean? But the other nine, where are they?"

We could flatten the story into the principle, "You must always be grateful for all things." Ingratitude is not acceptable, then or now. It is easy to stand back and judge the ungrateful nine lepers who failed to return. It is just as easy to fool ourselves into believing we are not like them, that of course we would go back to express our thanks. Yet in honesty, I wonder if I would really have turned around and gone back just to give thanks when I was well on the way towards my destination? Or would I have persuaded myself that a mailed thank-you card would be good enough? There is only one way to find out what I would really do: put myself in the story.

This story was not recorded in the Gospels merely to teach us a lesson on gratitude, even though it may do so. It is important to put aside our need to find principles and make quick applications for today. It is also important to put aside judgmental attitudes and even familiarity with the story.

Instead we need to come to the story as if for the first time and wonder about who we might be in the story and how we might respond in the inevitable encounter with Jesus. In order to do this more effectively, we need to put the story in context by asking basic questions. They are basic not because they are easy, nor because the answers are obvious, but because they require little, if any, self-reflection. Then we will move into deeper and more difficult questions that require critical self-reflection.

My first question: Why is this particular miracle story in this particular place in Luke's Gospel? This healing miracle has no obvious connection to what happens immediately before or after it. The story is placed in the midst of a long section that Luke has devoted to Jesus's final journey to Jerusalem. Only Luke records information about this final journey, and many of the stories and teachings in this section are unique to his Gospel.

The section begins with the revelation that Jesus knew his end was near and so "set his face to go to Jerusalem" (Luke 9:51).[1] There is a sense of deliberateness in this statement, a determination on Jesus's part to journey to the city, even though he knew he was going to be sacrificed for the sin of the world. It is the concept of journey that is significant. Throughout this long section, Luke repeatedly refers to the journey, which explains his abrupt introduction to our story, "On the way to Jerusalem. . . ." We are not meant to forget the journey Jesus was taking to offer himself as the sacrifice for sin.

The journey, while carrying literal significance, also has symbolic meaning. When I put myself in the story, I need to keep in mind that I too am journeying and will not arrive until the final climax—perfection in the new heaven and new earth. Each event along the way puts me one step closer, requiring responses of authentic faith to each encounter with Jesus.

Yet "keep the journey in mind" is hardly an adequate answer to my question about the placement of this account. The story of the ten lepers is truly oddly placed. In this journey to Jerusalem, Luke has gathered a variety of materials that includes both Jesus's words and deeds. His words, recorded in this section, are usually his response to a question, a comment, or even a criticism from a religious leader or member of the crowd. These direct teachings are interspersed with five healing stories with no explanation about any of them, not even why each healing story belongs in its particular stage in the narrative. We could be excused for thinking that Luke tossed all this information in the air and then placed it in the order that it landed, except for one thing.

Luke begins his Gospel with the claim that he has written "an orderly account" after careful investigation of all the facts (Luke 1:3). The order may not be obvious to us at first glance, but as New Testament commentator Michael Wilcock writes: "An exposition that discerns some kind of order, even here, is likely to be nearer Luke's mind than for which the passage is a rag-bag of scarcely connected episodes."[2] It is prudent to respect this claim of an orderly account, and therefore we can assume that Luke had a deliberate purpose in placing this story of ten lepers at this point in his Gospel.

This miracle of the lepers is the only miracle in the midst of a long passage that focuses on the words, rather than the deeds of Jesus. On either side of the miracle story there are parables and discourses. Suddenly Luke throws in a story that has no obvious teaching attached to it, and no relation to the teaching around it. No interpretation, no explanation. It is just there. I wonder why Luke put it there. What should we be noticing and reflecting on?

Luke—who is orderly and not random—deliberately placed this story between heavy teaching sections to get our attention. Perhaps he meant for us to sit up and take note of this important story, even though its importance is not readily observed. Perhaps we are meant to take this story as seriously as we take Jesus's teachings. Preachers, teachers, and commentators too often skip stories, preferring to focus on passages where Jesus is directly teaching. Why? These other passages are easier to put into point form for sermons and class lectures, and they are easier to find principles to moralize over. The placement of this story, therefore, lets me know of its importance. It demands our prayerful reflection and faithful response as much as Jesus's words.

My second question: Why does Luke, usually so sparse on detail, include detailed information about Jesus's geographical location when approached by the lepers? He tells us that Jesus entered a village in the region between Samaria and Galilee. The province of Galilee was in the north of Israel. Jerusalem, where Jesus was headed, was in the province of Judea in the south. In between these two lay the province of Samaria. The shortest way from Galilee to Jerusalem was through Samaria. Jews, however, usually took the long way, bypassing Samaria.

Jews, we are told by John, "do not associate with Samaritans" (John 4:9 NIV). Their prejudice against Samaritans was both mutual and old. It began after the Jews returned from Babylonian exile to their own land. By then, Samaritans had become a distinct ethnic and religious group, partly related to Jews and occupying land in Israel.[3] Their religion had some roots in Judaism. According to Jews, the Samaritans seemed to have taken from Judaism what suited them and mixed it with elements from other religions. The Jews despised them for their lack of ethnic and religious purity and considered them outcasts.[4]

Because Samaritans were considered outcasts, they were also considered ceremonially unclean, barred from entering the temple and practicing the rituals of worship. Most

Galilean Jews making their way to Jerusalem did so for the sole purpose of sacrificing at the temple, the only place for sacrifice. They could not afford to be made unclean by Samaritans, and so they took the long way round. No point arriving in Jerusalem and being unable to offer your sacrifice because a Samaritan had touched you and made you unclean.

Jesus was traveling to Jerusalem for the same reason as most Jews—to offer a sacrifice in the holy city, only he would offer the ultimate sacrifice: his life for ours. Of course, those traveling with him then did not know this. They knew he was going to Jerusalem in order to celebrate the Passover and would, therefore, need to be ritually clean. And yet Jesus chose to travel through Samaria, even entered a village that bordered both Samaria and Galilee. Obviously he would encounter some Samaritans there, and certainly he would become unclean according to the Jewish traditions of the day. No Jewish leader en route to Jerusalem for sacrifice and worship would have risked the contamination. Doubtless some wondered at Jesus's decision to travel through Samaria. Yet Jesus frequently confronted traditions, forcing people to question "why" and reflect on his true identity.

It was in this village between Samaria and Galilee that the lepers appeared. By giving us the geographical information, Luke has helped us enter the story with greater understanding, bringing our whole being, mind and emotions, head and heart, into the story.

Now we come to the penetrating questions that demand so much more from us personally. Put yourself in the story, identifying with one of the characters. Who would you be in this story? How would you behave? Would you have returned to give thanks? We each have to answer these questions for ourselves. I can only analyze my own life, write about my own responses in the hope that, in being personal, I will also be universal and relevant.

On the way to his destiny in Jerusalem, the lepers appeared. Not daring to get too close, they called out from a distance. "Jesus, Master," they cried together, "have mercy on us!" If you were one of those lepers, would you have kept your distance, or would you have dared to come up close?

It wasn't the Jew–Samaritan enmity that made them keep their distance. At least one of those lepers was a Samaritan. We can assume that the others were all Jews, which seems the implication of the text, even though we are never told. Here was a rare example of Jews and Samaritans freely associating together. They were all companions in disease. Together, they kept their distance because of their disease.

They were lepers, and both societal and Jewish laws demanded that they keep their distance. Moses gave some specific instructions about the treatment of lepers, because the disease was contagious. People with leprosy wore distinctive clothing, let their hair become disheveled, and warned others away by crying out, "Unclean, unclean." Lepers were ceremonially unclean and remained so until the disease was cured and a priest had cleansed them. To touch a leper, even accidentally, made a person unclean and incapable of participating in the temple rituals and sacrifices until seven days of ritual cleansing were completed. To avoid profaning the holy, lepers lived as beggars and outcasts on the outskirts of towns.[5]

These lepers were obedient to the Mosaic law, keeping themselves apart from those who desired to remain clean. But I also suspect they kept their distance to avoid the rejection and unkind comments of others, especially the religious Jews on their way to sacrifice in Jerusalem. They would naturally assume Jesus would want to keep himself uncontaminated from unclean people like themselves. While it was curious that Jesus chose to travel through Samaria, this did not seem to register with the lepers or make them think about Jesus's identity.

The lepers' behavior suggests at least two things to me. First, they were knowledgeable about their law and willing to obey it; they were a religious bunch. But second, they were not very knowledgeable about Jesus. They knew he was a healer, but they did not seem to know of his genuine compassion for outcasts. Neither could they have heard how he actually touched a leper once (Matthew 8:1-4). Instead of that leper making Jesus unclean, Jesus's touch cleansed and healed the leper. Had they known this, the lepers undoubtedly would have come closer and perhaps even touched Jesus.

Instead, they called out from a distance for mercy. I wonder what they expected Jesus to do for them. A prayer for mercy is not very specific. In another story, a blind beggar called out for mercy (Luke 18:35-43) and Jesus asked him to give a specific request: "What do you want me to do for you?" It seemed pretty obvious, but Jesus made the blind beggar spell it out. He did, with great faith: "Lord, let me see again."

Yet Jesus did not ask these lepers to get specific. There are times in our lives when it is impossible to pray anything more than, "Lord, have mercy." When I was rushed to the hospital with a severe reaction to chemotherapy, it would have been cruel to demand a specific prayer from me. I did not have the voice, and barely the energy to whisper, "Mercy." Likewise, these lepers had suffered greatly, both from the disease and from the cruel treatment demanded by the law and those who rigidly enforced it. Jesus would not make their life any more difficult. He heard their prayer and quickly responded, "Go and show yourselves to the priests."

The Mosaic law required no less, but only after the person was convinced of healing. A priest had to both verify the healing of a leper and then put the person through ceremonial cleansing for seven days (Leviticus 14:2-32). A leper only went to the priest if certain that healing had already taken place.

Luke does not make it very clear when healing actually took place for these ten lepers. He writes, "And as they went, they were made clean." Only *on the way* to Jerusalem did healing come. I wonder whether I would have obeyed Jesus without strong evidence of healing. Would I have headed for Jerusalem and the priests?

You probably also noticed that Luke used a word not normally used for healing. He writes that they were "made *clean*" rather than "healed" or even "made well" (as in verse 19). Luke has deliberately chosen a word we do not ordinarily associate with healing, and he uses it to mean both healed and ritually cleansed. This means that the trip to the priests was no longer necessary. The only reason they needed to go to the priests was for ceremonial cleansing. The verification of the healing was secondary. Jesus not only healed them, he also cleansed them, thus doing the priest's work.

It seems that only one leper recognized that the trip was no longer necessary, and he was a Samaritan. He was not supposed to know the law of Moses. He was an ignorant outcast. Yet he alone realized that both healing and cleansing had taken place. Because his disease was a skin disease, I suppose it was obvious to see the disease was gone and he was healed. But how did he know he had been made clean and the trip to the priest was now unnecessary? I especially wonder about this given my own experience with cancer.

My disease was neither visible nor obvious to me. I was totally ignorant of it until modern technology, X rays, and a biopsy revealed a small and slow growing tumor. Surgery was imperative. The surgeon successfully removed the lump and all the cancerous tissue surrounding it. We could verify the success of the removal of the lump and cancerous tissue through tests, but the doctor could not tell whether cancer had spread to other parts of my body. Chemotherapy was necessary.

On hearing this news, one of my students, visibly upset, came to visit me. The need for chemotherapy suggested to her that I was not fully healed, and she had been specifically praying for my complete healing. She wondered why God had not answered her prayer. I pondered this for a while, until I realized my disease was such that we do not really know whether I am fully healed or not. To this day, regular checkups remain a necessity. For this reason, if I were in the Gospel story, I wonder how I would know—immediately— that Jesus had both healed and cleansed me.

How was this Samaritan leper so sure of cleansing that could not be seen? Of course we could argue that, being a Samaritan, he did not really care about going to the priests. The cleansing ritual was not necessary for him. He was healed and that was enough for him.

Immediately, this "outcast" deserted his fellow lepers. He "turned back, praising God with a loud voice." He chose to keep company with Jesus rather than fulfill the religious and legal requirements. I like this Samaritan! Nothing could hold back his joy. It overflowed in enthusiastic praise to God as he made his way back to Jesus. This time he did not keep his distance. Coming as close as possible, he prostrated himself at Jesus's feet and publicly thanked him. This is the posture of worship before God. Did this foreigner realize Jesus's true identity as God? If so, he is one of very few who did. Even Jesus's disciples struggled with this until after Jesus's resurrection.

Jesus reacted with surprise and asked, "Were not ten made clean? But the other nine, where are they?" It seems that he expected all ten to return, to realize that the trip for cleansing was no longer necessary. He was amazed that it was the Samaritan, the lone foreigner (and even Jesus called him this) who came back to proclaim his gratitude. The other nine, pre- sumably because they were all Jews, he expected to return. But he did not expect a foreigner.

Jesus put aside his disappointment and publicly commended the Samaritan's faith. Then Jesus commanded him, "Get up and go on your way; your faith has made you well." Jesus approved the faith of a foreign outcast. This was important to Luke and probably one of the reasons why he alone included this story. Luke is the sole Gentile writer in the New Testament and was passionate about proving that salvation in Jesus was open to all people, not only Jews. This event was one more piece of evidence. Perhaps it was this concern for the salvation of the Gentiles that Luke remains silent about the nine who failed to return to offer their grateful thanks.

Why didn't they come back? I am always intrigued with what the Gospel does not record. So I examine the unexplained and unrecorded, not because I need answers about those ungrateful nine, but in order to keep company with Jesus, to become more like him. I was surprised at how easy it was to imagine myself being one of those other nine. As I reflected on their reasons for failing to return to Jesus in gratitude, I discovered a number of similarities with myself. "Would I return?" became a difficult question to ponder.

First, it seems these men were living in obedience to the Mosaic law as best they could. It was this very obedience that may have hindered their return. They kept their distance from Jesus and the crowds, avoiding the risk of making others unclean with their touch. They also seem to have understood exactly why Jesus sent them to the priests. They had knowledge of the requirements related to their healing. Without hesitation, they began the journey to Jerusalem and the priests. From this I think I can safely say that these nine were all Jews seeking to live in conformity to the law.

Were they perhaps too legalistic? If so, this would be a second possible reason for persisting in the journey to the priests; they were perhaps determined to obey the Law to the letter, even though Jesus, by healing and cleansing them, had made the trip superfluous. If they were indeed legalists, they could not, even if they had wanted to, return to Jesus before seeing the priest, such is the oppressive nature of legalism.

The Samaritan, who would have been despised by most Jewish people, had no such qualms. Nothing could stop him from publicly praising God and demonstrating his gratitude. The priests could wait! Our response to the Samaritan is positive. We like this guy. We have a tendency to judge the other nine rather harshly for their ingratitude.

I can also discern a third reason for their failure to give thanks. Unlike the Samaritan, these Jews were bogged down in their religious Jewish concerns, needing good theological proof. They were not sure Jesus was qualified to grant them cleansing. They really did not know him as anything more than an extraordinary healer. They needed theological verification of claims that Jesus was Messiah from leaders they trusted before committing themselves to Jesus's authority. The Samaritan, on the other hand, did not need this theological and biblical correctness. He was free to believe without approval from religious leaders.

There is still another possible reason why these nine did not—even could not—return. They needed greater certainty about their healing. They could not trust their own judgment. They needed the priest to examine their entire body and pronounce them cured. Perhaps, when they first approached Jesus, they hoped he would invite them closer. He did not. Neither had he touched them, pronouncing words of healing over them. There was no immediate visible evidence of healing. Nothing spectacular happened. How could they be sure unless a priest examined them thoroughly? And so I wonder whether they persisted in their journey to the priest because they needed verification of their cure. They needed greater certainty before they could accept this miracle.

I understand their reasons all too well because of my own experiences. In fact, in using my imagination to prayerfully reflect on reasons why the nine failed to return, I learned more about myself than about the lepers. And that is the point, to let scripture act as a mirror to help us come to the truth about ourselves. Keeping company with Jesus demands no less.

I too once struggled with a legalistic approach to obedience. Driven by that demanding "ought to" rather than a joyful "want to," I was more concerned with the letter of the law than with giving or receiving compassion and cleansing. I was more concerned with theological correctness, as it was interpreted in my Christian circle, than loving others. I was more concerned with acceptance by my religious leaders than being able to enjoy the freedom of believing in Jesus. Reflection on this Gospel story revealed truths about myself that I needed to name and own, and then to seek God's grace to overcome them.

Because I have also struggled with the need for certainty and verifiable proof, I dare not be dismissive and contemptuous of these ungrateful lepers. I have pity on them, knowing I would once have made the same choice as they did. I am sure they were thankful. They just lacked the freedom to show it. Transformation came into my life, not in one amazing event, but through painful self-discovery and grateful acceptance of God's grace to begin again "a new creation" in Christ (2 Corinthians 5:17).

The nine Jews were as healed and cleansed as the Samaritan. Like the Samaritan they remained cured, even though they failed to go back and offer thanks. Unlike the Samaritan, they missed out on hearing Jesus publicly commend them for their faith. They never learned that gratitude flows naturally from those who keep company with Jesus. Did they also live the rest of their lives ashamed of their ungrateful behavior? Jesus never meant for them to get to the priests. Hence his surprise that only one came back: "The other nine, where are they?" he wondered.

QUESTIONS FOR REFLECTION OR DISCUSSION

1. Jews once went out of their way to avoid Samaritans. What places and people do we avoid today fearing we could be made "unclean" or fearing we would risk our reputations?

2. Why do you think Jesus seemed surprised when only one leper returned to give thanks?

3. As you put yourself in the story, with whom do you most identify? Would you have made the effort to return to give thanks? Why or why not?

4. How can we each make gratitude—to God and to each other—a daily practice?

4. Ignored

Keeping Company with Jesus When He Remains Silent

MATTHEW 15:21-28

Jesus left that place and went away to the district of Tyre and Sidon. Just then a Canaanite woman from that region came out and started shouting, "Have mercy on me, Lord, Son of David; my daughter is tormented by a demon." But he did not answer her at all. And his disciples came and urged him, saying, "Send her away, for she keeps shouting after us." He answered, "I was sent only to the lost sheep of the house of Israel." But she came and knelt before him, saying, "Lord, help me." He answered, "It is not fair to take the children's food and throw it to the dogs." She said, "Yes, Lord, yet even the dogs eat the crumbs that fall from their masters' table." Then Jesus answered her, "Woman, great is your faith! Let it be done for you as you wish." And her daughter was healed instantly.[1]

I have always struggled with God's silence. As far as I am concerned, it is the most difficult trial to endure. Consider the story of faithful Job, who endured the loss of his family, wealth, and health. When he cried out to God in prayerful lament, God remained silent. Job would not have suffered nearly as much if God had only broken the silence. It was not easy for Job then and it is not easy for me today to wait out

God's silence. And yet it seems every child of God will, at some time in life, experience God's silence, that seeming absence of the presence of God. Because it is not unusual, I desire to know: How can I keep company with Jesus, God Incarnate, when he ignores me in a silence that is so loud?

Because I have experienced this often, I am drawn to a Gospel story in which Jesus ignored a woman and her plea for mercy. I struggle with this story, not only because Jesus ignored a woman *in need,* but also because he ignored *a woman* in need. The story reminds me of my experiences of Jesus's silence and my experiences as a woman in the church of Jesus Christ. I need to acknowledge these negative experiences. I could not maintain my integrity or be real in my relationship with Jesus if I were to pretend the story was all "glory hallelujah." I am forced to honestly come to terms with this story and the experiences it reminds me of. All the same, this story is one of the most difficult stories from Jesus's ministry for me to meditate on.

From one perspective, I understand Jesus's reaction to this mother who came begging for help for her daughter. He did not want to be disturbed. Mark is more explicit than Matthew in explaining this. He tells us that Jesus entered a house "and did not want anyone to know he was there" (Mark 7:24). This was not the first time Jesus had tried, unsuccessfully, to go "to a deserted place by himself" (Matthew 14:13), only to be tracked down by the crowds demanding his attention to their needs and wants. Even the scribes and Pharisees traveled all the way from Jerusalem in the south to Galilee in the north just to attack him with their test questions. Because Jesus could not get away in Israel, he left, going deep into Syria, "to the district of Tyre and Sidon." He desperately needed some alone time with his disciples. Perhaps he hoped that in the foreign region of Tyre and Sidon he would be unknown and therefore undisturbed.

It was not to be. Not even on foreign soil could Jesus remain undisturbed and, as Mark observed, "escape notice" (Mark 7:24). True, the Pharisees and scribes did not pursue him with their intentions to trick him once and for all. Neither did the crowd track him down to demand amazing words and deeds. Instead, Jesus's retreat with his disciples was disturbed by one alien woman in desperate need.

What did people think of her, a lone woman, daring to interrupt a famous Jewish rabbi's solitude and prayer? She had a few strikes against her that day:

She was from the wrong race—a Canaanite rather than a Jew, therefore considered unworthy of attention, if not an enemy.

She was the wrong gender—a woman instead of a man, which should have precluded her from interaction with Jewish leaders in public.

She was alone—she brought no man to lend her credibility. Perhaps she had no husband to protect and support her. As a single woman, she may even have been forced into prostitution in order to make a living for herself and her daughter; we do not know. If she was a prostitute, she was also unclean and untouchable.

Any of the three reasons alone should have excluded her from publicly approaching Jesus, a Jewish Rabbi. Yet despite all these strikes against her, the woman dared to speak to him, risking Jesus's reputation and her own. It must have taken great courage.

This is why I struggle so much with Jesus's response to her. It cost this woman to come to him and beg for help. Why did he then make it so hard for her? It's not as if she were all bad. She had some truly good points to her.

First, she knew who Jesus was and even where to find him. I wonder how? Jesus quietly came into Tyre and Sidon with his disciples, slipping deep into Syria unnoticed.

There was no demanding crowd flocking around to give his presence away. And, of course, there were no TV camera crews to announce his presence to the nation. Yet the woman recognized him. She may have seen Jesus before, possibly in Israel, and she may have been close enough to study his appearance, so she would to be able to identify him again. Maybe she had longed to talk to him in Israel but feared attack from Jews who despised foreigners and had little time for women, especially needy women. With Jesus now away from his home turf, the woman may have felt safe enough to come to him with her request.

Second, the woman not only recognized this man as the wonder-worker of Israel, she also knew he was the Messiah. She had no misgivings about bowing at his feet, as if before God.[2] In her petition, she addressed Jesus by his true identity, "Lord, Son of David," a familiar messianic title. This alien woman knew what few Jews knew then: Jesus was the Messiah, God's chosen savior. Even Jesus's disciples struggled with this truth. Some days they were so sure other days they were completely confused. One of those confusing days was the day Jesus calmed a storm at sea. In amazement and fear, they wondered, "Who then is this, that he commands even the winds and the water, and they obey him?" (Luke 8:25). In faith, the woman unashamedly and publicly expressed her belief in his true identity. How did she, a Canaanite woman, know? Where did her faith come from? Matthew does not tell us. We can only acknowledge this woman's second good point: she had faith that Jesus was the Messiah.

Third, she knew how to pray. With profound simplicity, she pleaded, "Have mercy on me, Lord, Son of David; my daughter is tormented by a demon." Because her petition is so basic and brief, you might be tempted to question my claim of her ability to pray, especially if you were taught, as I was, that good prayers are long ones, filled with many Bible verses and theological terms. Such prayers always intimidated me. I assumed they were proof of a well-developed faith, while my brief and simplistic prayers were evidence of my spiritual immaturity. (I have since learned that my belief itself—not the length of my prayers—was evidence of my immaturity!)

This woman's prayer, so brief and to the point, was enough, because it was prayed in deep faith and humility. It was a good prayer because, as the Jewish philosopher Abraham Heschel observes, "To be able to pray is to know how to stand still and dwell upon a word."[3] She knelt in stillness, dwelling upon her few repetitive words. All she wanted was mercy in the form of healing for her demon-tormented daughter. If this woman had no claim to spirituality, she certainly knew one of its most basic disciplines: prayer.

I can't help contrasting this story with a similar story also told by Matthew (Matthew 17:14-20). On that occasion, a Jewish father approached Jesus, bringing his demon-possessed son along with him. The similarity with the woman's story is obvious; they both had a child who was demon-possessed. But the parallel ends there. The differences are numerous. The second story is about a Jew, not a Gentile; a man, not a woman; a sick son, not a sick daughter. The father had so much more going for him than the woman, but it seems this father lacked the woman's good points.

First, he failed to identify and acknowledge Jesus as the Messiah and addressed him merely as "Lord," but more in the sense of "sir."[4] It was not unusual for women to express confident belief in Jesus's true identity. Martha made one of the fullest expressions of faith in her discussion with Jesus over the death of her brother Lazarus. In response to Jesus's question about her belief in the resurrection, she confessed, "Yes, Lord, I believe that you are the Messiah, the Son of God, the one coming into the world" (John 11:27). Yet we are more frequently reminded of Peter's confession: "You are the Messiah, the Son of the living God" (Matthew 16:16). Even Jesus's apostles, despite Peter's confident confession, struggled with the truth that Jesus was also God. Only after the resurrection did they boldly profess this. So this Jewish father was not alone in his hesitation to publicly identify Jesus.

Not only his faith but also his prayer stands in stark contrast to the woman's prayer and belief. Unlike the brief prayer of the mother, he talked at length about his son and their need. "Lord, have mercy on my son, for he is an epileptic and he suffers terribly; he often falls into the fire and often into the water. And I brought him to your disciples, but they could not cure him" (Matthew 17:15-16). The way we pray says something about what we believe and how we relate to Jesus. The woman realized that Jesus did not need a lengthy explanation in order to understand her problem; the father needed to describe the details. Unlike so many people then and now, the woman believed she would be heard even in a few words. Was she familiar with Jesus's warning not to "heap up empty phrases as the Gentiles do; for they think they will be heard because of their many words" (Matthew 6:7)? Clearly the Jewish father was not familiar with this warning, or with Jesus's assurance that "your Father knows what you need before you ask him" (Matthew 6:8).

On the other hand, the difference in their prayers could mean that the woman's need was far greater and, therefore, this was not the occasion to "keep on babbling like pagans" (Matthew 6:7 NIV). She was a woman alone in a society that made life oppressive for her. "Lord, help," is a perfectly good prayer at any time. I will keep using it.

As I compare the stories, I am surprised at Jesus's response in each case. The alien woman was at first ignored. The Jewish man immediately received his request. True,

Jesus was hard on the father, accusing him and the observing curious crowd of lacking faith, but then he immediately healed the son. The father, a Jewish male, was not ignored; the mother, an alien woman, was.

I do not understand Jesus's response. It is totally out of character for Jesus, at least the Jesus I learned about in the selective Gospel stories I studied in Sunday school and church as a child. Jesus was always so nice! He was the perfect gentleman, consistently polite, never saying the wrong thing, keeping conversation from getting too personal or too emotional. He was the consummate Mr. Nice Guy, that person who makes you feel good about yourself, always lending a helping hand at the first cry for help, willing to give a hug when your day is lousy, always available. This story shatters those pictures. How can I keep company with a Jesus who ignores needy women but not needy men? On the other hand, how can I keep company with a Jesus who is a figment of my imagination, based on my South African and British heritage and my American experiences? Meaningful company with Jesus demands authenticity. Therefore, we have to let ourselves be disturbed as we keep looking at this very different, even difficult picture of Jesus.

A desperate woman in need asked for mercy and Jesus, according to Matthew, "did not answer her at all." There were other occasions when Jesus first responded to requests with silence. Perhaps the most memorable is the story of the woman caught in adultery and publicly accused before a gawking crowd.[5] But I think I understand the silence on that occasion. The religious leaders who accused her behaved abominably and got what they deserved; Jesus ignored them. The silence was an opportunity for the woman's accusers to examine their own lives before condemning another. Jesus's silence on that occasion makes sense. But I see no obvious purpose in this silence. The woman came to Jesus with such faith and hope, but he silently ignored her. What kind of impression did this make on her? I can only imagine.

I know how the disciples felt because Matthew tells us: They were annoyed with the woman. They were concerned about their retreat with Jesus. It had taken a long time to find this undisturbed solitude that this alien woman was interrupting. As far as they were concerned, it seemed obvious that Jesus had no intention of healing the woman's daughter. Her persistent praying bothered them. As their patience quickly ran out, they urged Jesus, "Send her away, for she keeps shouting after us." They believed the best thing to do would be to send her away.

Yet why did they want to send her away empty-handed? Why didn't they urge Jesus to heal her? A request for healing would be more compassionate and free her to return home, leaving the disciples in peace. It would also be the request we would expect from those who lived daily in Jesus's company. Perhaps these Jewish disciples approved of Jesus's behavior and were relieved that for once he conformed to good Jewish religious custom by ignoring a woman in public.

I wish I could say with confidence that I would have been more compassionate, that I would have begged Jesus to show mercy and heal the woman's demon-possessed daughter, that I would not have behaved like those heartless disciples. But I do not know for sure. I do know that I once became angry with a needy woman who persisted in disturbing my solitude during a silent retreat. She bothered me with her silly questions, and I wanted her to go away. Why didn't I ask Jesus to have mercy on her? I do not know, and neither do I know why the disciples were so selfish. Reflection on this Gospel story forced me into repentance for my unkindness to the lonely woman who disturbed my silence.

If the woman's begging disturbed the disciples, it did not disturb Jesus. He allowed the woman to keep on praying, even though he ignored her. He did not help, yet neither did he put her in her "proper place" by silencing her and sending her home to her sick child. On the one hand, Jesus seemed to conform to Jewish religious expectations by ignoring the woman. On the other, he refused to dismiss her, as any good rabbi would do.

Although Jesus ignored the woman's plea for mercy, he did not ignore his disciples' irritated demand to send her away. He did not rebuke them for their heartlessness, which is what I would expect him to do. Instead, he explained to them that he "was sent only to the lost sheep of the house of Israel" and none other. The explanation is for the disciples, not the woman. But of course she heard it. Jesus seems to assure the disciples that he would not heal this alien and outcast woman. At least, his words suggest that. But behind Jesus's words was his behavior, which suggested something very different. He ignored her, but he also never sent her away. The disciples only noticed the ignoring and assumed Jesus was not going to help her. And so they thought that she might as well have been sent home. The woman noticed that Jesus neither sent her away nor did he flat out refuse to heal her daughter. There was a tiny glimmer of hope, and so she stayed, begging Jesus and bothering the disciples.

In his response to the disciples, Jesus suggests he could not heal the woman because of religious laws that would have excluded her on the basis of race. Yet if that were true, why didn't Jesus simply send her away the first time she begged? If he had no intention of healing her, why let her stay and continue her prayer? This incident is the only record in the Gospels of Jesus refusing to heal an alien and outcast. There are a few occasions when such people approached Jesus and each time he healed them; he did not use race as an excuse to ignore them. It is, therefore, surprising that Jesus ignored this woman on the basis of her being a Canaanite and not a Jew.

Even more surprising, the woman did not leave and neither did she stop praying. She waited out the silence. When Jesus responded to the disciples' request with those discouraging words, she again knelt before him and begged, "Lord, help me." I wonder what would have happened if she had walked away, understandably disappointed in the healer of Israel, on hearing his claim to help only the people of Israel? Would Jesus have called her back? I wonder, because I fear I might have given up, too hurt to remain, too proud to keep on praying. Would he have called me back?

It only got worse for her. Jesus did finally respond to her, but with what I think were the most uncompassionate words he ever uttered to anyone: "It is not fair to take the children's food and throw it to the dogs," he said. Why did he call this alien woman a dog? I confess I do not understand Jesus's racist comment. Because I believe racism is evil, I might have been tempted to rebuke Jesus! Or more likely, I would have returned home, bitter and angry, lacking the determination of this desperate mother.

Yet the woman persisted and was quick with a response: "Yes, Lord, yet even the dogs eat the crumbs that fall from their master's table." I admire her quick thinking. Even Jesus was deeply moved by her response and his compassion burst out. He proclaimed, "Woman, great is your faith! Let it be done for you as you wish." Her daughter was immediately healed. Mark tells us that she went home and found her daughter lying on the bed, demon free at last. Her persistence was worth it.

It was difficult, but she patiently waited until Jesus acted, and was then commended for her great faith. Yet I suspect she would say it wasn't her faith that kept her there. It was need; not her own need but her daughter's. Perhaps she would have given up in despair if the need were hers alone. For her daughter, she would have held firm when everything inside her told her to give up and go home. She would have endured anything—even being ignored and insulted. I can only assume she saw something in Jesus, despite his responses, that kept her hope alive. Jesus allowed her to stay, begging for mercy and, in the end, he healed her daughter completely.

There had to be a reason for Jesus's unusual behavior. Jesus rarely, if ever, did anything without good reason. And so I ask, who benefited from his silence?

Jesus was not the beneficiary of his behavior. He did not ignore her for his own sake. Jesus is perfect, completely whole, never needing transformation. Neither did he act selfishly. Selfishness would have prompted him to send the woman who interrupted his solitude packing. Being fully God, it was impossible for Jesus to act out of selfishness.

Neither can I imagine that the woman benefited from this experience. Jesus surely knew that he was expecting much from her as he ignored and then insulted her. Her faith was tested to the very limit. I wonder whether she became one of his followers afterward or whether she walked away grateful for her daughter's healing yet filled with sorrow and anger at the treatment she had received. Her faith was commended; her prayer was answered. But she had come with high hopes and had been tested to her limits. How, I wonder, could the treatment have been for her sake?

That leaves the disciples. It makes sense to me that they were the intended beneficiaries of Jesus's odd behavior. They had not been compassionate in any way toward this woman. She was bothering them. They probably despised her because she was an outcast—an alien, a woman, and perhaps even a prostitute. Never in their wildest dreams would they have imagined her capable of faith, even as small as a mustard seed. If Jesus had instantly responded to her request, the disciples would never have discovered her great faith. They learned an important lesson that day—even outcast alien women can exercise not just faith but "great faith." The silence was meant to force them to begin that transformation in their attitude and treatment of women and aliens. Jesus had great faith in this woman. He believed she would persist in her praying, and this persistence would give him an opportunity to demonstrate to his disciples what great faith looks like.

This lesson was not only for those disciples physically present that day. The story is for the benefit of all Jesus's disciples of all time. It is a constant reminder to keep on being transformed in the way we respond to aliens and outcasts and women. Her story has gone down in history, thanks to Matthew and Mark. Author Eugene Peterson called her "the marvelous Canaanite woman" and described her as having "bold simplicity, absolute lack of guile, and persistent directness."[6] And we don't even know her name! We never hear of her again, yet she will forever stand as a nameless woman who gives us all an example of great faith.

She also gives us an illustration of persistent prayer, an example to emulate. Jesus taught us to persist in prayer. Luke recorded a parable Jesus once told "about their need to pray always and not to lose heart" (Luke 18:1). This alien woman prayed and did not lose heart. Her simple prayer was repeated until Jesus responded. We need to learn from this woman to be faithful, indeed persistent, in prayer.

I have frequently experienced the absence of God that has tested both my faith and my willingness to persist in prayer. I take comfort from the psalmists who often complained about God's absence in laments such as "Why, O Lord, do you stand far off? Why do you hide yourself in times of trouble?" (Psalm 10:1). Praying the psalms has helped me keep my faith in those experiences of God's long silences. And so I think I understand why this nameless woman patiently waited for Jesus to respond with healing for her child.

I have also experienced attitudes in the church very similar to those of the disciples, attitudes that complain (in actions more often than in words), "She's bothering us." From an early age I was taught that women must keep silent in the church. The teaching insidiously implied that women are inferior to men, and I was ashamed about being an intelligent woman. When I felt called by God to minister as a Christian educator in the church, no less than two pastors said to me, "If you were a man with these qualifications and experiences, I would hire you immediately." Again I felt inferior.

As I reflect on reasons why the woman remained praying in Jesus's presence, I assumed it was because she saw or even felt something the disciples missed. When I wondered about why I remained in the church, eventually riding above feelings of inferiority and insignificance, I realized it was because of something I saw and felt in Jesus: his compassion and respect that taught me of my significance; his forgiveness for my sin and the grace to forgive those who hurt and hindered my journey. Like the woman's daughter, I too experienced healing and was grateful that I had kept begging.

It is difficult to remain faithful and stay with Jesus in his silence, that seeming absence of his presence. But maybe a great lesson is in the making, a lesson that only Jesus's silence can reveal. And maybe the lesson is not for me alone but also for other followers of Jesus. Will we keep the faith and persist in his company? And will he be able to publicly commend us for our great faith? I can only hope so.

As I continued to reflect on this story and Jesus's behavior, I had to admit that maybe the silence was for the sake of the alien woman after all. Jesus was deliberately hard on her to bring her to the realization of her faith. She might have said her need, rather than her faith, kept her there. Jesus saw it differently. Need always brings out great faith. Because Jesus ignored her and because she courageously persisted in praying, she heard those wonderful words of commendation. Despite how she felt, her faith was enough and would help her endure Jesus's absence after he returned to Israel, and even after he returned to glory. Perhaps she did become a faithful follower of Jesus after all.

This explanation forces me to think again about my pictures of Jesus. I have let go the images of the perfect gentleman and the Mr. Nice Guy and replaced them with more truthful impressions. This is the challenge the story presents to us all. Jesus cannot be expected to fit our molds. Jesus might come to us in ways that we feel insult us. He may even ignore us. And each time he will do it for our sake, in order for us to discard our false concepts of him, helping us to continue growing in our relationships with him. He is willing to risk our angry pride in order to bring us into a more intimate relationship with him. If we desire to keep company with Jesus, we can expect that he will rebuke us in ways that may hurt; he will not make us feel good about ourselves when we are in the wrong; but he will always help us find truer images of himself and of ourselves. I therefore keep praying, "Help me, O Lord, to keep letting go of false images of you in order to take on truer pictures that bring me closer to you. Amen."

▦ ▦ ▦

QUESTIONS FOR REFLECTION AND DISCUSSION

1. Compare Matthew's account of this story with Mark's (7:24-30). Note differences and similarities and discuss what these suggest about each author's intentions for recording this story.

2. How have you experienced the absence of God and how have you responded to that? In what ways does this story help you find ways to face God's seeming absence in the future?

3. Describe the picture of Jesus that you see in this story. How does it make you feel, think, and wonder? What response do you think Jesus is looking for from us today?

5. THE MAN WHO DID NOT WANT TO BE HEALED

When Keeping Company with Jesus Is Downright Puzzling

JOHN 5:1-18

After this there was a festival of the Jews, and Jesus went up to Jerusalem.

Now in Jerusalem by the Sheep Gate there is a pool, called in Hebrew Bethzatha, which has five porticoes. In these lay many invalids—blind, lame, and paralyzed. One man was there who had been ill for thirty-eight years. When Jesus saw him lying there and knew that he had been there a long time, he said to him, "Do you want to be made well?" The sick man answered him, "Sir, I have no one to put me into the pool when the water is stirred up; and while I am making my way, someone else steps down ahead of me." Jesus said to him, "Stand up, take your mat and walk." At once the man was made well, and he took up his mat and began to walk.

Now that day was a sabbath. So the Jews said to the man who had been cured, "It is the sabbath; it is not lawful for you to carry your mat." But he answered them, "The man who made me well said to me, 'Take up your mat and walk.'" They asked him, "Who is the man who said to you, 'Take it up and walk'?" Now the man who had been healed did not know who it was, for Jesus had disappeared in the crowd that was there. Later Jesus found him in the temple and said to him, "See, you have been made well! Do not sin any more, so that nothing worse happens to you." The man went away and told the Jews that it was Jesus who had made him well. Therefore the Jews started persecuting Jesus, because he was doing such things on the sabbath. But Jesus answered them, "My Father is still working, and I also am working." For this reason the Jews were seeking all the more to kill him, because he was not only breaking the sabbath, but was also calling God his own Father, thereby making himself equal to God.

Keeping company with Jesus through Gospel stories is frequently puzzling, and nowhere is this more evident than in this story of the man who did not want to be healed. Two things in particular puzzle me about this story: first, that Jesus bothered with the man, and second, that John included a story that at first glance does not have anything to do with his stated purpose. Of all the Gospel writers, John is the only one who clearly states his purpose in writing—"that you may come to believe" (John 20:31). I am puzzled because this man seems to have little to attract Jesus's attention, and the story seems to be more about unbelief than faith. What on earth does this story have to do with helping us believe? How can it, I wonder, help us in our desire to keep ever more meaningful company with Jesus?

I will begin with the man who was healed. As we progress through the story, we discover, as Lesslie Newbigin in his commentary on John's Gospel points out, that he "has nothing to recommend him except his need."[1] Why did Jesus choose to heal this person in the first place? He is described to us simply as a man "who had been ill for thirty-eight years." With no explanation about his illness, his background, his personality, we can only make assumptions about him as we enter the story and examine the text, remembering this will teach us as much about ourselves as this chronically ill man at the pool.

The text makes it clear that he had been at the pool for a long time and that he had trouble getting into the pool on his own. This would suggest that the man was either unable to walk or walked with great difficulty. It is possible that, with so much lying around at the pool, his muscles had atrophied, further restricting movement.

Another fact we know about this man is that he did manage to get to the pool, perhaps on a regular basis. He had good reason for coming to the pool. It was a popular belief that in certain seasons an angel of God would touch the waters of the pool; the first person into the pool after the waters were stirred up would be healed. Later manuscripts of John's Gospel added a verse that explained this phenomenon. In our Bibles today, this is either listed as verse four or as a footnote. According to Culpepper, "John 5:4 is a textual gloss that explains that after an angel stirred the waters the first one in the pool would be healed. The verse does not appear in the best manuscripts, and it does not appear in any manuscript before the fifth century."[2] The fact that the man had made attempts to enter the pool suggests to us that he did indeed desire to be healed, that he even had a plan for his healing. He believed in the magical powers of those waters. His plan for healing was to wait at the pool and be the first one in when it was stirred.

Of course, for us today this all sounds very unscientific and rather superstitious and futile. But he lived in another era, when people believed in miracles rather than science, believed in angels who periodically—unannounced and unknown—

touched the water at the pool, believed that being the first one in the pool caused miraculous healing. John does not bother to refute or confirm the validity of this man's belief. It could have been an actual angelic healing or just a powerful mythological or psychological belief. As Sanford writes, "It is entirely possible that people had such faith in this [event] that certain persons entering the water at this time were healed, so strong can be the influence of *psyche* and *soma*."[3]

Whether miraculous or psychological, the man believed that healing could take place in this pool. His problem was that in all those years he had lain there, he had never managed to make it to the pool in time. How many times had the waters been stirred while he waited? Why had he missed each opportunity for healing if this was his only plan? If he truly desired healing, wouldn't he have waited at the edge of the pool? This is why I wonder about this man and even why Jesus bothered with him.

I think of him as a tragic figure. His belief in those stirred waters kept him at the pool called Bethzatha despite the fact that he could never reach the water in time. He had no one to help him into the pool and made no other plan for healing. He is a sad contrast to the paralyzed man in the story Mark tells, whose friends carried him to Jesus to be healed (Mark 2). As the man in John's Gospel explained to Jesus, he had no one to help him. I wonder why he never perched himself as close as he could get to the pool. If he really wanted to be healed, he could have found a spot to wait at the very edge, easy to roll in when the water moved. Having been there a long time, you would think he would have some rights to the best spot, from which it would have been easier to make the trip to the water before anyone else. He seems to have stayed too far away to win the race to the pool. I think there were a number of things the man could have done if he really wanted to be healed. He did not do any of them and neither could he be honest about his true desire to remain as he was, an invalid.

It is not easy to live a healthy life at any age. Healthy living demands working hard, taking responsibility for ourselves and perhaps a few others, being disciplined, and avoiding unhealthy habits. I have occasionally met people who avoid taking responsibility for their health; they are always looking for another doctor, another counselor who will tell them what they want to hear. To me, it seems this man at the pool did not really want a healthy life with all its responsibilities. In a sense, he chose to remain in his unhealthy state instead of doing what was needed to change.

Then Jesus came to Jerusalem for one of the Jewish festivals. In John's narrative, this was only his second visit to Jerusalem, coming after a period of ministering north in and around Galilee. He probably was relatively unknown in the city and thus was able to make his way unhindered to the pool of Bethzatha, around which crowded dozens, maybe hundreds of chronically ill people. Here Jesus had an opportunity to decisively make his name known and remembered in Jerusalem. I have no doubt that he could have healed all of those people immediately. He could have touched the water and invited every "blind, lame, and paralyzed" person there to dive in for healing. What fun the Jerusalem newspapers would have had with that one the next day! But as always, Jesus resisted the spectacular and disappointed people, just for a moment.

Ignoring all the other ill people waiting patiently for an angel to stir the waters, Jesus picked out this one man and walked over to him. What attracted Jesus to this man? The author of John merely writes that Jesus "knew that he had been there a long time" but fails to tell us how Jesus knew that. Was this evidence of Jesus's divine powers, his ability to know without being told? Did others point out the man as a tragic figure? We do not know for sure.

The man must have been surprised when Jesus, a total stranger, came up to him and asked, "Do you want to be made well?" It seems like a silly question. I imagine Jesus's followers were thinking, "Isn't that obvious?" Here the man was, sitting by the pool, waiting for the miracle. Yet Jesus asked the simple question—which required a very simple yes-or-no answer—and this man could not give a simple reply. Instead, he explained to this stranger why he never made it to the pool on time. It wasn't his fault he was still ill. He had no friends to help him. Others always beat him to the pool. It seems he was doing his best to absolve himself of responsibility. Why doesn't he answer, "Yes, sir, I want to be made well"? Perhaps, knowingly or unknowingly, he does not want to be made well. Perhaps he is afraid.

Jesus did not ask the question because he needed an answer. If he knew the man had been there for a long time, he also knew that the man had repeatedly tried and failed to be healed. I assume he also knew that—consciously or unconsciously—the man did not really want healing. That is what I find so puzzling about Jesus's behavior. There probably were sick people there that day who truly did long for healing. Jesus ignored them all, focusing his attention on the one person there who did not seem to want his attention and help.

Jesus already knew the man's answer. The question was for the sake of the man himself. It was a question intended to force him into an honest self-examination, to discover the true desires of his heart. Did he really want to be made well? Was he prepared to engage in honest self-reflection? It would seem he was not. Rather than answering Jesus's question, he expounded on his problem with attaining health.

The question is also for you and me today. We too need to hear Jesus ask us, "Do you want to be made well?" We may not have a physical ailment, but we all struggle toward wholeness as we deal with physical, emotional, and spiritual incompleteness. Do we really want to be made well? If so, what are we doing about it? After honest self-reflection, how would we answer Jesus's question?

At this point in the story, Jesus would probably not have disappointed this man had he turned to one of the other many needy people lying around the pool that day. I wonder why he didn't. Why did he bother with this man and all his excuses? Then I see myself in this pitiful figure, complaining about my lot, failing to take on the responsibilities of my life, and I am grateful that Jesus did bother. The story assures me that he will keep bothering with me. I can be sure that I will never hear Jesus say, "Take Jackie away. She's bothering me!" And I am relieved and grateful.

Jesus ignored the man's complaining and with authority commanded, "Stand up, take your mat and walk." It was not a suggestion. The abruptness of the command makes me wonder whether perhaps Jesus was just a little impatient with this man who refused to engage in self-reflection when given the opportunity. I am afraid I would have become annoyed. I get angry with myself when I have behaved in ways not too different from this complainer. In the end, I am thankful Jesus loves me enough to rebuke me abruptly and surely.

I suspect that the man was caught off guard. Without thinking, he stood up, picked up his mat, and walked away. He obeyed Jesus to the letter. A moment's reflection, however, and he perhaps would have started arguing with this stranger, explaining that walking would be impossible for at least two reasons. First, he had been ill for thirty-eight years. It would take months of physical therapy and training to get those atrophied muscles working again, if ever. Second, it was the Sabbath. Though we learn this only after the fact (verse 9), the man knew it. Jesus had just asked him to violate the Sabbath rules to avoid all work, which included works of healing and carrying your bed through the streets. If he were a good Jew, nothing would make him violate the Sabbath law. If he had been given time to reflect, I think he would have preferred to remain an invalid at the pool rather than break the Sabbath rules, especially in public where others, including the religious leaders, would see.

But it was too late for reflection. The man was healed, and he walked away, carrying his mat and breaking the Sabbath. He did not even pause to thank the stranger who had healed him nor did he ask his name. The man walked off and straight into trouble. "The Jews" stopped him, reminding him, "It is the sabbath; it is not lawful for you to carry your mat." They harbored no joy for a man who was finally well after so many years of sickness; instead they rebuked him.

"The Jews" are an interesting group in John's Gospel. They were the conservatives who, like many conservatives, resisted change, even good change. As in this story, "the Jews" most often refer to the Jewish religious leaders, usually called "the scribes and Pharisees" in the Synoptic Gospels, Matthew, Mark, and Luke. But there is another meaning. "The Jews" in John are not necessarily Jewish by race but all those who refused to believe that Jesus was the Messiah, those who rejected him and did not become Jesus's followers. Because it was mostly the Jewish religious leaders who rejected Jesus, John's Gospel usually uses the term "the Jews" to refer exclusively to them. In many ways, they represent what Newbigin calls "established religion."[4] They remind us of the dangers of maintaining dead traditionalism, mistaking it for the life-giving traditions of the faithful past.

"The Jews" stand in contrast to a second group of people John called "disciples." The disciples represent all those who believed in Jesus as Messiah and committed to faithfully following him. They do not, in John's Gospel, refer exclusively to the twelve Apostles. John called all followers of Jesus "disciples," be they women or men, Jew or Gentile. They are examples of those who put their faith in Jesus and thus support John's purpose. It is not surprising that John included them in a story, since his purpose was to evoke belief in Jesus. What is surprising is that John also included examples of negative reactions to Jesus.

"The Jews" experienced Jesus in similar ways to "the disciples." They heard his teaching and marveled at its ring of truth and authority. They saw the different miracles and were amazed. There was just one major difference—their response to Jesus. We might expect John to have included only stories of disciples, because they believed in and received Jesus. But John shocks us by including accounts of those who rejected Jesus. This is so unlike much of our evangelism today. We try so hard to make the gospel appealing to the masses that we avoid stories of those who reject Jesus and instead go overboard with stories of those who believe.

This brings me to my second question. Why did John include a story that seems to have little to do with evoking faith in Jesus? The healed man is the first example in this story of a person rejecting faith in Jesus. As he walked away carrying his mat and met the religious leaders, he again failed to take responsibility for his actions on that particular Sabbath. This time he blamed "the man who made me well." Naturally the Jews asked who healed him. Who was this man who believed he had authority to command another to break Sabbath rules? The man replied, "I haven't a clue."

Unbelievable! For thirty-eight years he needed healing. He probably dreamed about it and talked about it; certainly he waited for it. A stranger gave him what he desired, and the man never bothered to ask his name. True, Jesus quickly disappeared into the crowd. But the man was well and could now walk; he could have gone looking for Jesus. Even though his religious leaders did not know Jesus, surely there were people who did. Only when smarting with the rebuke from his religious leaders for breaking the Sabbath law did the man realize it was important to know who had healed him.

Maybe the man did not want to know Jesus, but Jesus wanted the man to know him. The healed man needed an opportunity to make a decision about Jesus. The stories of Jesus are not bedtime stories to make us feel good and give us a good night's sleep. They demand a response, a decision to follow or reject Jesus. So Jesus again initiated contact with this man. He found him in the temple and warned him, "See, you have been made well! Do not sin any more, so that nothing worse happens to you."

It might appear here that Jesus was equating sin and sickness, blaming the man's illness on his sin. This was a traditional view. Even today we might be tempted to believe that sickness is a result of specific sin in our lives and that healing is a simple matter of genuine confession of sin. We would be wrong. In another story, the writer of John tells us about a man who was born blind and healed by Jesus. The disciples, who accepted the traditional view, ask Jesus whether it was the man's or his parents' sin that caused his blindness from birth. Jesus was quick to respond, "Neither" (John 9:3). Sickness is not necessarily directly related to a specific sin. We all suffer and die because we live in a fallen and sinful world.

However, it does seem in this story, as Sanford suggests, "that in Jesus's mind the man's sin and his illness were connected."[5] His sin was the refusal to take responsibility for healthy living, pretending he wanted to be well while all the time doing little to actually become whole. Jesus would have none of this. He healed the man and then commanded him to live a healthy life or worse would befall him. And the man's response? He remained ungrateful. After discovering Jesus's identity, he immediately hunted down those religious leaders who had rebuked him earlier and betrayed Jesus to them.

It seems the man refused to believe in Jesus despite personally experiencing a miracle. John does not explicitly say this, but he was usually so quick to bear witness to faith we can assume there was none in this case. In the story about the man who was born blind, John recorded his unequivocal declaration of faith: "Lord, I believe" (John 9:38). The fact that no such declaration appears in John 5 leads me to believe that the man healed in Bethzatha joined the group John called "the Jews" rather than "the disciples." The man rejected Jesus, refusing to believe despite the evidence.

I am sometimes tempted to think that if only God would perform more miracles today, more people would believe in Jesus. John's story reminds me this is not true. Miracles—or signs, as John calls them—do not necessarily promote faith. In fact, they may have the opposite effect. We can neither demand nor expect a miracle to magically increase our weak faith. We are responsible to do the hard work of reflecting on Scripture in ways that teach us about Jesus and about ourselves. The miraculous signs that affirm our faith in Jesus are mostly in the ancient past, recorded in Scripture for our instruction. Keeping company with Jesus does not mean we should demand or even expect frequent miracles. In fact, Jesus once rebuked the crowd, saying, "Unless you see signs and wonders you will not believe" (John 4:48).

The religious leaders are another example of rejection and refusal to believe in Jesus. Not only didn't they believe, but they also became antagonistic towards Jesus. John lets us know that the healed man's betrayal of Jesus began the persecution of Jesus by the religious leaders. They were so bound by their legalistic adherence to their narrow interpretations of the law that Jesus was seen as a major threat, undermining and setting aside the law. They rejected Jesus because he failed to live according to their standards of keeping the Sabbath holy and because he practiced what they concluded was blasphemy. When they finally met Jesus and confronted him about his behavior, Jesus only made matters worse for himself. He boldly called God "My Father." This, in their eyes, was claiming equality with God, and therefore was blasphemy, deserving condemnation and death by stoning.

Unbelief comes when we least expect it. Who would ever have thought that the recipient of a miracle would reject Jesus? But he did. And who would think that the representatives of the religious order would reject Jesus? But they did as well. Keeping company with Jesus can be downright puzzling at times. As I meditated on this story of a man who did not want healing and then made no confession of faith, I questioned and wondered. And then I realized I was focusing on the wrong thing. This is not really a story about a chronically ill man. It is a story about Jesus. The miracle of the man's healing is a sign that points to Jesus. Signs are placed to direct our attention elsewhere. When I travel, I search for the signs to point me to my destination. It would be very strange to stop at a sign and go no further. Signs point the way. They are not the way itself. John tells the story of an ungrateful recipient of Jesus's healing who failed to confess faith in Jesus in order to point us to Jesus himself. The sign affirms our faith in the one who called "God his own Father, thereby making himself equal to God."

⊠ ⊠ ⊠

QUESTIONS FOR REFLECTION AND DISCUSSION

1. Why do you suppose Jesus deliberately sought out this man rather than any of the others at the pool that day? Imagine the possible lesson Jesus might have desired his disciples to learn.

2. The chapter suggested that by making little effort to be healed, the man did not want to be healed. What makes it easier (in some cases) to live in ill-health rather than seek a healthy resolution? What do you think is needed to live whole and healthy lives today?

3. This story points to the truth that Jesus is fully God. How should that truth affect our relationship with Jesus and help us relate more meaningfully to him?

6. At the End of the Day

Keeping Company with Jesus in Unemployment

JOHN 21:15-19

When they had finished breakfast, Jesus said to Simon
Peter, "Simon son of John, do you love me more than
these?" He said to him, "Yes, Lord; you know that I love
you." Jesus said to him, "Feed my lambs." A second time
he said to him, "Simon son of John, do you love me?"
He said to him, "Yes, Lord; you know that I love you."
Jesus said to him, "Tend my sheep." He said to him the
third time, "Simon son of John, do you love me?" Peter
felt hurt because he said to him the third time, "Do you
love me?" And he said to him, "Lord, you know everything; you know that I love you." Jesus said to him,
"Feed my sheep. Very truly, I tell you, when you were
younger, you used to fasten your own belt and to go
wherever you wished. But when you grow old, you will
stretch out your hands, and someone else will fasten a
belt around you and take you where you do not wish to
go." (He said this to indicate the kind of death by which
he would glorify God.) After this he said to him, "Follow me."

At first this story may not seem to have much to do with
unemployment. On the contrary, Peter is given work,

sent out as a servant of Jesus Christ into active, daily employment. This is surely the last story an unemployed person
wants to read. Peter, whose résumé left much to be desired,
was given employment, while those with impressive references and experience waited around fruitlessly. Trust me, no
unemployed person would deliberately choose to read this
story. I was unemployed and unwittingly read it.

A few years ago I lost my job, but I wasn't the least bit
worried at first. I had spent ten years teaching in higher edu-
cational institutions, and I was finally enjoying it. It had
taken me those ten years to realize that teaching was my
vocation, not just a job. I was content at last, rejoicing in the
recognition and ownership of this truth about myself. I was
one of the privileged ones, doing what I enjoyed and what I
was called to do. Why should I be concerned when my teaching job fell through because the seminary was forced to
make budget cuts?

"Never mind," I consoled myself. "God would never help
me recognize my vocation, realize I was actually in it, and
then take it from me. I will have no problem finding another
position as a college professor." Without stopping to reflect,
I sold most of my possessions, packed up what remained,
moved to the United States, and eagerly began my job
search. It is probably just as well that I never knew what lay
ahead for me. Today, with the wisdom of hindsight, I know I
should have taken time out for prayerful reflection—not
reflection on what I should do next or where, but on a much
more important question, maybe the most important question: At the end of the day, what really counts in life?

If you had forced me to pause as I busily packed up my
stuff and asked, "Jackie, what in life really matters?" I would
not even have slowed down as I responded, "What really
counts in life is my love for Jesus. What I do, how much I
accomplish, the good goals I achieve, will count for very little

compared with my loving Jesus with my whole heart. *Being* (that is, who I am) is much more important than *doing*." And, if you were interested, I would have gone on to explain that I do not mean "doing" is unimportant. Neither do I mean that we are meant to simply sit in some trancelike state, focusing on who we are. The point is that what I do always comes out of who I am. If I focus on loving Jesus, building my relationship with him, what I do will become more and more Christlike. If I focus on doing alone, it will quickly become oppressive and meaningless. That is what I would have told you the day I lost my job.

At the time, I did not bother to pause for reflection because I was so sure I knew the answer and had often confidently taught it to my students. A few months before losing my job, I was again reminded of that answer as I studied this text in John for a sermon. Yet in hindsight, my wild dash to find another teaching position clearly illustrated that while I may have known the answer in my head, I did not know it in my heart. The gap between what I claimed to believe and how I lived was vast. Unemployment would reveal exactly how vast.

Suppose you could have been a fly on my wall, watching my behavior as my unemployment stretched out longer and I became more distressed. You would have disagreed with my answer and thought, "Jackie believes that doing—being busy for God, being in the right teaching position—is what really counts at the end of the day." I had no idea of the conflict that existed between my behavior and my heart's belief. I was about to learn, thanks to months of unemployment.

I did not get another job immediately. A year went by and I was still unemployed, with no prospects of finding a job. I discovered my behavior contradicted what I confidently claimed to believe. As unemployment stretched into months of nothingness, I became angry with myself and with God. My self-image plummeted to an all-time low. Without work accomplishing tasks for the kingdom, I was nothing. So much for my claim to believe that being and loving Jesus is more important than doing and having. I rushed into the job market little realizing that I still needed work and possessions to give me my identity. I was so sure my focus was on how much I loved Jesus, so sure I had left behind my emphasis on doing and having. I was so wrong. I was finally forced into the reflection on what mattered.

Unemployment opened my eyes. With little to do, each day was empty, and I felt worthless. I accomplished nothing of significance, so I concluded I had no worth and no identity. I came to the sad realization that work—making a difference, earning a salary, paying my own way, driving my own car, living in my own home, possessing numerous sets of keys—were all essential parts of my true identity. Doing and having were more important to me than being and loving. Long months of unemployment stripped me bare.

I know I am not alone in believing that doing is more important than being. I see it all around me. Our contemporary Western culture emphasizes doing not being. What we achieve, how much we accomplish, how successful we are in terms of producing results counts for so much in our modern world. And I am not just talking about the non-Christian world. The emphasis on the active life is very much part of our churches. It is rare to be asked, even by Christians, "Do you love Jesus?" We are more likely to wonder what was done for the kingdom today, how many people we witnessed to. As the well-known spiritual writer Henri Nouwen observed, "Being busy has become a status symbol" in contemporary society.[1] When asking another for help, it is not unusual to preface the request with, "I know you are busy, but. . . ." We often find it jolting when a person responds, "No, I'm not busy. In fact, I have absolutely nothing to do at the moment." People who have nothing to do are often considered failures.

By admitting we have time to do nothing—and in fact doing just that—we risk losing the respect of others. So it is not surprising that in my unemployed state, I felt like a failure, ashamed of what people would think of me. Losing my job did not bother me much, at least not after the initial shock. Staying unemployed month after long month did. My situation was becoming downright treacherous as I was confronted with my naked self, alone in the presence of God. I was shocked to discover that I still lived as though I believed that the active life is the only worthwhile life.

This belief, affirmed by society, had been reinforced in my years as an active church person. I learned to emphasize doing as a teenager, encouraged by a saying attributed to missionary William Carey, whose story I discovered at a young age: "Expect great things from God. Attempt great things for God." For us teens, the emphasis was not on *expect.* That was all together too passive, likely to lead us into trouble. We focused on *attempt,* seeking out ways to be actively involved in doing works for God, rather than spending time in prayerful solitude before God.

This belief was also reinforced in my college and seminary training. I received more training in techniques—the active side of ministry, such as preaching, teaching, administration, counseling—than in personal spiritual formation and holy living. In the church we sometimes measure spiritual maturity by how involved a person is in church activities. We are frequently surprised and shocked when an active Christian leader falls into sin, thinking that his or her work for God was a sign of spiritual maturity. We wonder, How could such a person have failed?

We live as though the only question God will ask of us at the end of the day is, "What did you *do* for my kingdom?"

Because we want to give a good answer, our lives are filled with activity. What we do to ensure that we will succeed and accomplish great things dominates our lives far too much of the time. Doing becomes ego-driven, giving us good feelings about ourselves. When that is all taken from us in unemployment, or by some other thing such as illness, we flounder with feelings of worthlessness. At least I did.

Even though I struggled with unemployment, I continued my daily discipline of keeping company with Jesus in the Gospels. Each morning, before I entered the day, I would meditate and pray from a Gospel story, systematically and leisurely working my way through the Gospels. Eventually I came to John 21 and the story of Jesus's encounter with Peter on the beach after the resurrection—which is after Peter's major failure, his denial of Jesus. And that is why this is, for me, a story about unemployment.

Unemployment forced me into serious reflection about what really counts in life, indeed, even in death. This was exactly what Jesus was asking Peter to do in this story. Despite the fact that I knew the story so well—I had even preached on it—I had missed an important aspect of it, indeed, the one aspect I should have paid attention to when I lost my job and rushed into the job market. I failed to notice that Peter was in the same position as myself—unemployed.

Peter and his brother Andrew had been in a reasonably lucrative fishing business with their father until Jesus walked by and commanded, "Follow me." Mark's Gospel claims, "And immediately they left their nets and followed him" (Mark 1:18). They quit their jobs! For the next three years their "business" was following Jesus. Then Jesus was crucified, and Peter was unemployed. Not sure of the way ahead, Peter did exactly what I did; he avoided time out for prayerful reflection and rushed back into the one job he knew. He returned to his home turf, Galilee, to fish. What else was he supposed to do? He could not sit around doing nothing. In that moment of great uncertainty after Jesus's death and resurrection, Peter needed the certainty of the familiar around him. He was not alone; a few of the other disciples went with him.

It was a waste of time. All night out in the boat on the Sea of Galilee and "they caught nothing" (John 21:3) until early in the morning when Jesus appeared on the beach. At his command, the catch was instant and generous. Breakfast that morning was fresh fish grilled on the beach. And they enjoyed the meal.

After breakfast Jesus turned to Peter, singling him out from the others. He had work for Peter to do, but first he must be sure that Peter understood what really mattered. Addressing only Peter, Jesus asked three times, "Simon son of John, do you love me?"

Now I grew up with this story, so before my unemployment, I saw only what I already knew about it. To be honest, I was a little bored with the story and too busy to pay close attention to it. I was also too blind to observe what was actually there in the text, until I became unemployed. Now I had all the time in the world. For the first time I began noticing details in the story I had missed in the past, details that ultimately prepared me for eventual employment.

Three times in this story Jesus addressed the fisherman Peter as "Simon son of John." Not once did Jesus use the name he himself had given him: "Peter." This seemed rather strange to me. Upon checking other parts of the Gospels, I discovered that Jesus most frequently used the name "Peter"; only rarely did he call Peter by his full name. I concluded there must have been a specific reason for Jesus to address Peter by his old name, using it exclusively and repetitively. It is a reason the Gospel writer does not reveal. This means that we have to use our prayerful imagination, recognizing that what we discover will say more about us and our relationship with Jesus than offer a correct interpretation of the passage. But that is what we need in order to keep company with Jesus—better knowledge of ourselves and of Jesus.

"Simon son of John" is Peter's full name. "Simon" was the name his family gave to him at birth. "Son of John" indicates his heritage, the equivalent of a surname in Western cultures. The first time Jesus met Peter, he said to him, "You are Simon son of John. You are to be called Cephas," which translated as "Peter" (John 1:42). Much later, after Peter made that climactic statement concerning the identity of Jesus as Messiah and Son of God, we discover the significance of the name change: "Peter" means rock, and Jesus saw him as a rock in his church (Matthew 16:18). "Peter" was his new, given name—his *Christian* name, if you like. I imagine that for Peter at least, it signified the new life he now had in Christ. He liked being called "Peter" and was probably upset when Jesus insisted on calling him by his old name, the name that took him back to his past. Before Peter would be ready for his new employment, even before he could honestly reflect on Jesus's question, "Do you love me?" he had to be taken back to his roots, to who he really was. I think this is what Jesus intended that morning on the beach when he called Peter "Simon son of John." Jesus desired that Peter respond from his *true* self rather than his *false* self.

My true self is who I really am. It is the person I was when I came into this world and was named; it is the self I will be when I stand before my Creator and Redeemer at the end of my life. My true self is the person God sees and desires for me to know and be.

We all have a true self, yet sadly, few of us know who we really are because we have developed a false self that is more comfortable and familiar. The false self is made up of the masks we put on to hide and protect the true self. These masks develop at an early age for numerous reasons. Masks are related to what we do, what we possess, and even what we feel, which are usually the ways we use to describe ourselves. For instance, when asked who I am, I most frequently respond by describing what I do for a living. As we grow older, we often mistake our masks for our true selves. This was the lesson Peter was about to learn on the beach at Galilee.

I believe that up to this point in his life, Peter had operated from the false self, the self that needed to please, needed to present a good front, needed approval. I have been there myself. In my early years, I promised to follow God even if it meant going to some out of the way place as a missionary. But in reality I was not prepared to go off as a missionary. I was only desperate for approval from those around me. Even years later, the day I rushed into the job market, I was so convinced that I was going about it the right way, that is, focused on who I am before the Lord. But I was still operating from the false self and never knew it.

The evening of Jesus's arrest, Peter confidently claimed his willingness to die with Jesus (John 13:36-38). He was operating, with so much bravado, from his false self. Moments later when the soldiers arrested Jesus and took him away, Peter, along with the rest of the disciples, also fled. And out of all the disciples, only Peter disowned his Lord three times (Mark 14:66-72). His brave claim to die with Jesus, not unlike my promise to be a missionary, had come from the false self. We can never make good on these claims, as Peter discovered, and as I did also during unemployment.

That morning on the Galilean beach, Jesus addressed the true Peter, "Simon son of John," and at long last the true self responded. His recent failure of denial had taught Peter a painful lesson about himself. Gone was the bravado and thoughtless promises. In true humility and integrity, Peter now stood before Jesus. And this is exactly the way Jesus needed him to be.

Peter had to hit rock bottom to get there. And so did I. Unemployment was a dark and seemingly bottomless pit that kept getting deeper and darker. I did not know at the time that I needed to be there to hear Jesus address me and then to be able to respond as my true self.

There could also be another reason for addressing Peter as "Simon, son of John." Jesus was using his full name. There are few occasions—my baptism and graduations come to mind—when I am addressed by my full name, "Jacqueline Lyddell Smallbones." There are important documents—my birth certificate, passport, tax returns, bank accounts—that bear my full name. Occasionally when people addressing me want my full attention—either because I have been ignoring them or because they have something important to say— they use my official name. So perhaps Jesus wanted to get Peter's attention, because the question was indeed serious, not to be answered superficially.

With this sense of seriousness and formality, we should expect Jesus to ask an important question. The circumstances were critical. Jesus was about to return to his father. His disciples were about to begin their ministry in Jesus's name, and Peter would play a crucial role as a key leader. This was a time for big, important questions. And Jesus simply asked, "Do you love me?"

Jesus's question is neither the one we expect to hear nor desire to answer. If we are honest, we should admit our surprise. In our technological age we might even consider this an irrelevant question, having nothing to do with how we are going to get the job done. We are not trained to answer such a question; we are better prepared to respond to questions about our qualifications and intended goals and plans. "Do you love me?" is an ontological, or "being" question, and we are far more comfortable with behavioral, "doing" questions. Jesus's question takes us beyond superficial externals and deep into our soul. This is the very question our active lifestyles help us avoid. We would likely avoid Jesus's question by posing our own logical and relevant questions.

Peter was being commissioned to go out and preach the Gospel, making disciples of every nation—the ministry that has been handed to the church today. All Jesus asked of him was love. Had we been present, we might have asked him about his goals for reaching the world for Jesus and his plans to ensure success. Had his commissioning occurred in modern times, we would have sent him to seminars on time management, goal setting, and evangelism and seeker-sensitive preaching techniques. We would have encouraged him to pursue a seminary degree to improve his preaching and disciple making. So intent on attempting great things for God's kingdom, we fail to see the importance of just being, of simply loving Jesus.

Instead of being concerned about our accomplishing great things, Jesus asks about our being, our relationships. It does not make sense to our contemporary culture. In the fifth century, St. Augustine understood this point and audaciously claimed, "Love God and do as you please." He recognized that life begins with this important relational question: Do you love Jesus? What we do will have meaning only if it is done from our growing love relationship with Jesus Christ. Our acts of service must flow out of our love relationship with Jesus. At the end of our lives, Jesus will not ask, "What did you do for me?" He will ask, "Do you love me?" Will we be prepared to answer?

Because the question is so important, Jesus did not ask it before his arrest. He knew Peter needed to fail and fail badly before he would ever be willing to answer with integrity. I believe I know how Peter would have answered before Jesus's crucifixion. In a sense, after the last Passover meal with the disciples, he actually does answer this question, even though Jesus did not ask it. Jesus warned all the disciples that night of his impending death and that they would all desert him. Peter alone refused to accept this, confidently claiming, "Even though all become deserters, I will not." Jesus was forced into warning him that before morning, Peter would deny Jesus three times. Again Peter was quick with his reply, "Even though I must die with you, I will not deny you" (Mark 14:29-31). From that background, I believe Peter's answer to Jesus before his arrest would have been an unequivocal, "I love you enough to die for you." The immediate future for Peter would demonstrate that not only was he unwilling to die with his Lord, he was also too willing and too quick to disown him.

As Peter stood on the beach that morning with Jesus, his memory was filled with that painful experience of disowning Jesus. He was at his most vulnerable. This was the right time for Jesus to ask, "Simon son of John, do you love me?" Jesus used the Greek word for love, *agape.* In English we might put the question like this, "Do you love me enough to sacrifice your all for me, enough to die for me?" Peter responded using a different Greek word for love, *phileo,* which means brotherly or familial love. In essence, Peter says, "I love you because we're family." Peter's true self is speaking. The bravado has been shattered. He stands in naked truth, and his answer is rather weak. Even Peter knows that, which is probably one reason why it hurt when Jesus persisted in asking the same question.

Peter knew from his recent denial that he was not prepared to die for Jesus. He even lacked the courage to admit that he was a follower of Jesus when Jesus needed him most. The true Peter could not claim agape love, even though Jesus gave him three opportunities to do so. Peter could offer far less than Jesus asked from him.

For this reason Jesus's response to Peter is amazing. After each of Peter's weaker answers, he commissioned Peter: "Feed my lambs," "Tend my sheep," and "Feed my sheep." Jesus did not look at Peter's weak answer and disqualify him from ministry. The fact that Peter could not love with a sacrificial love at that point did not mean he was excluded from ministry in the kingdom. Jesus kept him in. There was still room for a Peter who failed to rise to the required standards. Jesus further affirmed Peter when he switched to Peter's meaning of the word for love: *phileo.* At this stage, it was not important to Jesus whether Peter could love sacrificially, with a willingness to die for him. It was important that Peter could be honest. Humility, with its accompanying integrity, is necessary for all who desire to keep company with Jesus. Because Peter lacked insight into his true self before the crucifixion, he could claim sacrificial love. But Jesus did not send Peter out into ministry on that occasion. Instead, he warned of failure. Likewise, when we fail to recognize and respond as our true selves, there is no authentic ministry for us. We too will fail.

The true self is often less than perfect. I can put on a perfect mask for my friends. In fact, I have often done so. Through my busyness, I tried to show the church, my bosses, and even God that I was perfect, that my love for God was indeed selfless and I was willing to give my all in ministry. But that response came from my false self and was a lie. The true self does not make deceptive claims because integrity is important. That is what Jesus most wanted and got from Peter after his humiliating but necessary failure. Subsequent history demonstrates that, in the end, Peter did grow into loving Jesus sacrificially. According to tradition, Peter was crucified upside down. He chose to go upside down, because he considered himself unworthy to die the same way his Lord had died.

That morning on the beach after breakfast, Peter still had a long way to go. I believe he succeeded in the end because he was willing to answer with integrity, as his true self. This is what relationship with Jesus is all about. It could mean confessing that we are not as spiritually mature as we would like to think, that we cannot at this stage of our lives love Jesus sacrificially. From the depth of my unemployment pit I could not offer sacrificial love. I was too angry to even pretend. I could only love Jesus, and then just barely, because "we're family." The truth about myself finally came out. And I discovered, as Peter did, that being honest and admitting our weaknesses does not exclude us from relationship with or service for our risen Lord. In fact, when we are at rock bottom, honesty is all that is needed to grow in that relationship. Once we get that right, the rest will follow in ways that could surprise even us. Who would have thought that Peter, the big-mouthed fisherman would one day be crucified upside down for his Lord? But he was. At the end of the day, Peter had what counts—he loved Jesus with his whole self.

Even though I gained this understanding, I was still not yet ready to leave the story. I felt there was more to see and know. Not only was the question serious, it likely was presented to Peter alone. John does not give us much detail at this point; I can only imagine that Jesus took Peter aside. Perhaps the others were eavesdropping; perhaps they were talking among themselves. We do not know because the writer does not say. We do know that Peter had to answer alone, that no one else could do it for him. Solitude with Jesus was essential in order to hear Jesus speak and then respond with integrity.

One of the major problems with our busy lives, and perhaps the reason we are so busy, is that we are rarely alone with Jesus and so never hear the question and never discern the true from the false self. For each of us, there comes a time to be alone with our Lord to hear him address us personally. Only when we are alone can we recognize the true self and own the false. Perhaps many of us never answer Jesus with integrity, never even hear the question, because we never take time out to be alone with him. Unemployment was that essential alone time for me, forcing me into truth about myself and my relationship with Jesus. Only after that was I ready to be guided into new employment. The position I accepted after long months of unemployment was one I would have refused to even entertain the day I lost my job. It was not the position I believed I was called to. The solitude unemployment forced upon me was essential to discover my true self and hear God's call to teach college rather than seminary students. As always, God's call is so perfect.

I can't imagine that Peter felt very comfortable as Jesus drew him away from the others and talked alone with him. In fact, Peter eventually tried to shift Jesus's attention to the other disciples, asking, "What about John?" (John 21:20-22). Should we try to do the same, we will also hear Jesus's loving, "Mind your own business!"

When our time comes, how will we answer the question, Do you love me? Will we be prepared to go into solitude, allowing Jesus to address our true self? The true self likely will not be able to promise great things, as Peter did before the crucifixion. Our honest answer might be less than Jesus asked—family love rather than sacrificial love. It is enough, because in the end, our love relationship with Jesus is all that matters and will transform our love into sacrificial, self-giving love. At the end of the day, will we have what really counts?

■ ■ ■

QUESTIONS FOR REFLECTION AND DISCUSSION

1. Describe experiences you may have had of being alone with Jesus that forced you to face Jesus with integrity. What did you learn about God and about yourself?

2. What, as you perceive it, gives most people around you their identity today? How would they describe themselves? How do you describe yourself?

3. Why is the question, "Do you love me?" a seemingly irrelevant one in today's culture? How can it become our most important question?

4. Prayerfully reflect on ways you can take time out of your busy schedule for meaningful solitude with Jesus.

7. "WHO TOUCHED ME?"

Keeping Company with Jesus in Sickness

MARK 5:24-34

And a large crowd followed him and pressed in on him. Now there was a woman who had been suffering from hemorrhages for twelve years. She had endured much under many physicians, and had spent all that she had; and she was no better, but rather grew worse. She had heard about Jesus, and came up behind him in the crowd and touched his cloak, for she said, "If I but touch his clothes, I will be made well." Immediately her hemorrhage stopped; and she felt in her body that she was healed of her disease. Immediately aware that power had gone forth from him, Jesus turned about in the crowd and said, "Who touched my clothes?" And his disciples said to him, "You see the crowd pressing in on you; how can you say, 'Who touched me?'" He looked all around to see who had done it. But the woman, knowing what had happened to her, came in fear and trembling, fell down before him, and told him the whole truth. He said to her, "Daughter, your faith has made you well; go in peace, and be healed of your disease."

I once believed I would never suffer with breast cancer. From the stories I had heard as a child, I came to see it as the most dreaded disease for a woman. I feared it and tried to convince myself it would not happen to me. After all, I had always been a healthy person, living a reasonably healthy lifestyle. There was no history of breast cancer in my family and hardly any of the long lists of possible causes for breast cancer applied to me. Because I was so convinced I was immune, I was very slack about regular breast examinations.

As I lay on my hospital bed recovering from breast cancer surgery, I thought about how dumb I was to think I was immune. I remembered the Gospel story of the woman who had known serious suffering and dared to touch Jesus's clothing for healing. I wondered why she secretly touched Jesus's clothing rather than simply asking to be healed. I also wondered what I would have done had Jesus come to my town.

The story of the woman's encounter with Jesus is told not only in the Gospel of Mark but also in Matthew and Luke, suggesting its importance.[1] She is one of those minor characters in the Gospels from whom we learn much about Jesus and ourselves. Her story is our story, even though it was not this woman's intention to be a figure from whom others would learn. The woman did not set out to encounter Jesus. Her goal was to avoid public and personal contact with him. Who was she to disrupt the plans of a busy teacher and healer?

As Mark makes clear, Jesus was busy. He moved swiftly from one event to the next with a sense of destiny. He never stayed in the same place for long; first he went to this side of the Sea of Galilee and then the other. Recognized by all as a healer and teacher from God, he was sought by all for his gifts. This woman saw a man too busy to be interrupted; he was also unlikely to be in her part of the country for long.

This was her only chance for healing, yet she did not really have a plan, only faith in his power to heal her of an incurable disease.

The day Jesus came to her area, "a large crowd followed him and pressed in on him." The woman's problem became how to get through the crowd and close enough to the healer. Asking permission to approach Jesus and request healing was impossible for her; had the disciples known of her condition, she would not have been permitted to come close to Jesus. Because of her perpetual bleeding, she would have been considered ceremonially unclean, and along with lepers, she would have been shunned by all and barred from religious observances. As New Testament scholar William Lane comments, "A woman suffering from this complaint was called a *zabah,* and came under the restrictions of Leviticus 15: 25-33."[2] Any person who touched her or even anything she touched immediately became unclean. Unclean people were forbidden to enter the temple and participate in temple rituals of worship. For twelve years she had been an outcast, excluded from the community at worship and shunned by her religious leaders.

How different her situation was from that of Jairus, the synagogue ruler, who had captured Jesus's attention quite easily. His story surrounds the story of the unnamed woman in Mark 5 (see verses 21-24 and 35-43). Jairus flowed through the curious crowd, confident and unhindered. The crowd willingly gave way to this respected synagogue ruler. He kneeled at Jesus's feet, begging Jesus to come to his home and heal his dying daughter. Jairus and this nameless woman could not have been more different. He had a number of social and religious advantages she lacked: He was a man; she was a woman. As the synagogue leader, he was an important person in his society; she was an outcast. He was not suffering with an unclean and therefore untouchable disease;

she was and therefore was barred from entering the synagogue. He was respected; she was shunned. He presumed
Jesus would drop everything and come to his home; she presumed Jesus would avoid her.

Jairus's faith in Jesus's power to heal is obvious. He fell
down at Jesus's feet—the posture of worship—and acknowl-
edged Jesus's superiority. He humbly begged on behalf of his
only daughter, who was twelve years old and near death.
"Come and lay your hands on her, so that she may be made
well, and live," he pleaded (Mark 5:23). The laying on of
hands was common practice in Judaism. Lane writes, "What
was unusual was his confidence that if Jesus would come, his
daughter's life would be saved," unusual because healing
rarely resulted from the rabbinic laying on of hands.[3] Jairus
expected Jesus to heal his daughter and had no qualms about
diverting the busy healer. He assumed Jesus would drop
everything and respond to his plea for help. It was not necessary, he reasoned, to bring the child to Jesus. Naturally
Jesus would come to his home, regardless of the inconvenience to himself, his disciples, and the following crowd.

And he was correct. Without a word, Jesus went with him.
So did the crowd, giving him little room to move. Yet no one
wondered or complained at this sudden change of plans, not
even the disciples—and, as we know from other stories, they
were not beyond complaining or reminding Jesus of local
custom. Remember the Canaanite woman who came alone to
beg on behalf of her only daughter? At first, Jesus ignored her,
and the disciples begged him to send her away. This was their
way of reminding Jesus that rabbis did not have to attend to a
woman who came without a man to lend her credibility.[4] But
when Jairus, a respected man and a religious leader, delayed
them on account of his daughter, not one of Jesus's disciples
protested. Presumably it was acceptable for a man, especially
a synagogue ruler, to interrupt and monopolize Jesus's time.

I sometimes wonder what their response might have been had the request for diversion come from this nameless, oppressed woman rather than an important man like Jairus. Women in general were not highly respected in Jewish culture, and this woman in particular was shunned because of her illness. At that time, most religious leaders enforced the Mosaic law regarding uncleanliness with merciless rigidity.

Twelve years is a long time to be an outcast. The very people raised up by God, to stand between her and her God, refused to come near her and pray for and with her. Naturally she assumed she would receive similar treatment from Jesus. He too was a Jewish rabbi—true, he was very different from the rabbis she was acquainted with, but he was still a rabbi. How could she be sure that he would treat her any differently?

Given these cultural traditions of the time, it is not surprising that the woman lacked the confidence of Jairus. Plus there were the crowds to hinder her, and Jesus's disciples often tried to screen the people wanting healing. Along with that, Jesus was on his way to heal an important leader's child. It is no wonder she made no attempt to publicly announce her presence and request healing. Yet her faith in his ability to heal her was very real.

The woman was desperate for healing. She had spent all her money on a medical profession that failed her. Her only hope for healing was Jesus, the Teacher-Healer. And he was finally nearby, on her side of the Galilean Sea. She had to act quickly, while she had a chance at all. In her mind, she quickly formulated a plan. "If I but touch his clothes, I will be made well," she reasoned within herself as she slipped unnoticed, even undaunted, through the crowd. Unlike Jairus, who asked Jesus to come to his home to heal his child, touching his garment was sufficient for her faith. If Jairus was a man of faith, she was a woman of great faith.

I have put myself in this story many times since I went through my struggle with breast cancer. Each time I identify with the woman, not Jairus, as I cannot understand his calm assumption that Jesus would drop all at his request. I do understand the woman's reluctance to approach Jesus.

I also relate to the woman's affliction, even though the details of my story are very different. She had suffered with hemorrhage after hemorrhage for twelve long years, with no relief from her medical team. In contrast, my diagnosis happened all too quickly: On Wednesday I learned I had cancer; on Monday I had surgery. I had no time to process the diagnosis during those few days because I was forced to face a difficult decision: Do I have a lumpectomy, with the possible risk of not removing all the cancer, and then endure the inconvenience of daily radiation for seven weeks in a city an hour away? Or do I have a mastectomy, thereby avoiding radiation while making sure that all the cancer cells are removed? As I agonized over that decision, I had to inform people about my situation. My family, my friends, my employers, my students—they all needed to know. I made my decision, told the necessary people, and went in for surgery; all of this happened without time to process the diagnosis. It was still difficult and painful to say, "I have breast cancer."

The unnamed woman in our story endured her problem for twelve years. From the time I went for that routine mammogram until the time all the treatments were over, I had suffered a mere five months. True, it felt like twelve years, and it did take a few years to regain my full strength. But after a mere five months, I was no longer actively dealing with the disease. I cannot identify with chronic pain and expensive but fruitless visits to numerous doctors. Others can, but not me.

My recovery moved quickly because I had a competent medical team who immediately diagnosed and treated my disease correctly. State-of-the-art medical equipment, a highly qualified medical staff, and good medical insurance were all on my side. Mark tells us that this woman "had endured much under many physicians, and had spent all that she had; and she was no better, but rather grew worse." Luke, in his account of her story, is a little less judgmental of the medical profession. He admits that she had spent all her money, and then merely states that no one could cure her (Luke 8:43). My story is so different.

Yet I still identify with this woman and wonder how I might have approached Jesus. I wonder whether my knowledge of Jesus would have hindered or helped me. Would I have had the confidence, instilled in me by my faith community, to confront Jesus openly and boldly, or would I have plotted to be healed secretly, unnoticed by Jesus or the crowd?

I suppose there were many reasons why this woman chose to touch the fringe of Jesus's garment (Luke 8:44), rather than ask for healing. As I recovered from surgery, I thought I understood why: She wanted to maintain her privacy! Twelve years of doctors had forced her to give up too much. She wanted to protect what little anonymity she had left. That is how I felt after just three days in the hospital. Prodded, poked, and forced to reveal all, I longed to have my privacy back. As I reflected on this story, I naturally at that time read my own longing for privacy into the woman's act.

The truth is, we do not know why she came to Jesus secretly. The Gospels fail to address the issue. I am glad, because it is another invitation for us to use our imaginations, to put ourselves into the story. When we do this, the story challenges and transforms us, as it helps us to encounter Jesus, the Son of God, in fresh ways, keeping ever more joyful company with him.

There are two possible reasons for her secretiveness. She was a woman, and she had a ritually unclean disease.

If the woman approached Jesus boldly and confidently, would he respond? And if he did, if he were to reach out and touch her, wouldn't she make *him* unclean? Perhaps one of her goals in being secretive was to protect Jesus from her unclean state. How was she to know that Jesus, the sinless Son of God, could never be made unclean and instead could clean her of both disease and sin? She probably did not know about the leper Jesus touched and made clean. That experience did not make Jesus unclean (Luke 5:12-14). Out of respect for Jesus and his position as a rabbi, she might not have wanted to ask him to touch her. She seemed determined to act privately, unnoticed even by Jesus.

When I learned I had breast cancer and needed surgery, I didn't immediately go to the church to find people to talk to about my dreaded diagnosis, but not because I feared their reaction. Instead, I went home and—true to my British heritage—made a pot of tea. I cried my way through the entire pot. Then I went to church to talk to my pastor. Thankfully, I live in a different time than the woman with the twelve-year hemorrhages. I had no fears that I would be brushed off because I was a woman interrupting a busy man. My pastor did not scream, "Unclean!" He did not rush me out of his office and out of the church. There was no merciless rigidity from the man who stood that day between God and myself. And yet I was still reluctant to confess I had breast cancer. In that respect, I identify with this nameless woman. It took courage for me to tell my pastor I had cancer.

Under Mosaic law, I suspect cancer would have been considered unclean. Cancer is a monstrous imperfection, an unwanted enemy; having it is frightening. Deep down, I think this is why I feared public confession. Admitting I had cancer was tantamount to admitting I was imperfect. Of course I know I am—I came to terms with the truth of my own sinfulness and imperfection long ago. I have learned to laugh at myself when I make mistakes and otherwise fail to achieve perfection. But like many people, I grew up with a need to be perfect in order to be accepted, and this remains an issue I regularly deal with. Still it surprised and even shocked me that I was so reluctant to say publicly, "I have breast cancer." My pastor even had to talk me into allowing him to pray for me during church service on Sunday. I was embarrassed and reluctant to publicly announce my disease.

I also relate to the idea that the unnamed woman probably felt second-rate. I grew up in a church that treated women as inferior to men, and occasionally I still come across such churches today. Would such a community have encouraged me to approach Jesus publicly, as Jairus was able to do? Probably not. Had I remained in that atmosphere, I too would have remained hidden, incapable of coming forward, even for prayer. I too would have likely sought healing secretly. I understand this woman's desire for secrecy.

Somehow, she made her way through that demanding, pressing crowd. How many people did she touch and make unclean as she slipped by? As New Testament commentator, David Gooding remarks, "Religious people in the crowd could have been angry with her for mingling with them and thus infecting them with her uncleanness."[5] Her secrecy was essential. They must never know that she slipped through them on her way to Jesus. At last she reached Jesus and touched the hem of his garment. "Immediately," writes Mark, "her hemorrhage stopped," and she felt, deep within, that she was healed and cleansed.

"Immediately," writes Mark again, "Jesus turned about in the crowd and said, 'Who touched my clothes?'" He was aware at once that power had departed from him. This is the only occasion Scripture records when Jesus felt power leaving him. Although difficult to interpret, it probably reflects the true nature of Jesus as both fully God and fully man, living on earth under the authority and control of the Father.[6]

The disciples were cynical. "You see the crowd pressing in on you; how can you say, 'Who touched me?'" Commenting on this, Lane writes, "Their impatience with the Lord reflects an awareness that their immediate mission was to assist a girl who was dying, and delay could be fatal. It also betrays that they had no understanding of what had taken place."[7] Jesus ignored them as he kept searching the crowd for the one who touched him for cleansing and healing. I love the way Mark records this: "He looked all around to see who had done it." It gives a sense of Jesus's urgency to know who touched him and to make the deed public.

The woman's heart sunk—this was not supposed to happen. No one was ever supposed to know. Once she was safely home, she would likely have told a few close friends, but that was all. How was she to know Jesus would feel power leaving him the moment she felt power entering her? There was nowhere to hide, and Jesus kept looking all around. Did their eyes meet? I wonder. I can picture her coming forward "in fear and trembling." Her private and secret act was now public and open. With courage and gratitude she told Jesus, with the crowd listening in, the whole story, as Jairus, no doubt impatient, waited his turn.

Her fear was replaced with joy as Jesus, with deep compassion, announced for all to hear, "Daughter, your faith has made you well; go in peace, and be healed of your disease." Jesus called her daughter in recognition that she belonged in God's family. Her faith, a woman's faith, was seen by Jesus and publicly commended.

Despite Jesus's commendation, there are still a number of biblical commentators who fail to give the woman credit for her great faith. In his commentary on Mark, author Donald English suggests that the woman's faith was simple, and even superstitious.[8] Lane concludes that she probably believed, as did others, that "the dignity and power of a person are transferred to what he wears," and thus her faith was combined with "quasi-magical notions."[9] Lane goes on to argue that by forcing the issue into the open, Jesus made sure the woman realized "it was *the grasp of her faith* rather than her hand that had secured the healing she sought,"[10] as though the woman were too inferior to know that. In contrast to these scholars, I appreciate Gooding's assertion that "she was healed because hers was genuine faith and not mere superstition."[11] She knew what would happen if she but touched the hem of his garment. Her faith in Jesus's power to heal was truly profound.

I often wonder why Jesus stopped and demanded, "Who touched me?" Was it because he genuinely did not know? He was both fully God and thus omniscient, yet fully human and thus finite in knowledge. It is possible he did not know. But I believe it wasn't for his sake, for the satisfaction of his curiosity, that he asked the question. He called out the woman and made her story public. In doing so, Jesus taught her that faith in him can never be an impersonal "touch-his-clothes-only" faith. It requires a personal encounter with the living Christ. Jesus gave the woman this great gift of a personal touch, the gift of keeping company with him even in sickness. She took it with fear and trembling, but also with joy. She discovered that unlike some people in her faith community, Jesus treated women and men as God created them—equal in God's image.

It is easy to draw the conclusion from Jesus's commendation, "Your faith has made you well," that healing is a result of the sick person's faith. Many religious people today teach that if sick people "only believe," or "just have faith," they will be made well. I do not deny the importance of faith in the healing process. But I know from other Gospel stories that faith was not always present in the sick person healed by Jesus. Jesus healed the man who had been ill for thirty-eight years and lain at the pool at Bethzatha *despite* his lack of faith. The man did not even know who Jesus was. He was never commended for his faith.[12] The blind man described in John 9 was also ignorant of Jesus's identity; he likewise had no faith in Jesus when Jesus restored his sight. Faith came after the healing and discovery of Jesus's identity.

No, healing requires something more than our faith. That something is the sovereignty of God. It is God's wisdom that determines whether we are to be healed or whether we are to live with the problem. In fact, I think it requires greater faith to live with the problem than to receive healing, even miraculous healing. Twelve years with an incurable disease had forged a faith in the woman with perpetual bleeding. Her faith helped her know she would be healed merely by touching his garment. In contrast, Jairus had no such certainty. He needed Jesus to come to his home and touch his dying daughter himself.

Jairus was never commended for his faith. While he waited for Jesus to identify and then affirm this nameless woman, his daughter died. The servants asked him, "Why trouble the teacher any further?" Jesus overheard and assured the father, "Do not fear, only believe" (Mark 5:35-36). Such encouragement was needed to bolster a floundering faith. On reaching Jairus's house, Jesus demanded a private ceremony. The nameless woman's healing needed to be out in the open; Jairus's daughter's return to life was private, and the response from Jairus and the few who saw the miracle was amazement.

I wonder about my faith. Would Jesus say to me today, "Your faith healed you"? I do not know. I am not even sure I am fully healed. After all my treatments, I had to ask my oncologist how to describe myself. I wondered whether I should say, "I *have* cancer" or "I *had* cancer." He replied, "You are a cancer survivor." Was it faith that brought me to that place? If it was, it was not my faith alone.

The greatest lesson I learned from my ordeal with cancer and its brutal treatments was to rest in my community of faith. There were days when chemotherapy made me too weak to pray anything more than the occasional lament, "My God, my God, why have you forsaken me?" (Psalm 22:1). Chemotherapy does that to its victims. Yet my faith community prayed for me. They kept company with Jesus for me when I was too sick to care. And when chemotherapy made me too weak to care whether I lived or died, my community fought for my life on my behalf. I am a cancer survivor because I live within a community of great faith.

In one sense, I am more fortunate than this lone, nameless woman. When my courage and faith failed me, my faith community stood with me and supported me through the entire ordeal of cancer and its treatment. And yet this woman has a courage and faith I greatly admire and long to possess. I too hope to hear Jesus say to me: "Daughter, your faith has made you well; go in peace, and be healed of your disease." Perhaps one day he will.

◼ ◼ ◼

QUESTIONS FOR REFLECTION AND DISCUSSION

1. Compare Mark's version of this story with Matthew's (9:18-26) and Luke's (8:42-56), noting differences and similarities. Reflect on what each writer seems to emphasize and what this suggests about why this story was so important.

2. How do you perceive the attitudes of your church toward serious illnesses, such as cancer or HIV/AIDS or chronic depression? What difference does the person's gender or status in society make? In what ways do these attitudes encourage or discourage victims of disease from seeking help in the church today?

3. Since much of what Jesus said and did was intended to train his disciples, what lessons do you think his disciples learned from his responses to Jairus and the woman? What lessons do you learn to help you keep more faithful company with Jesus?

NOTES

CHAPTER 1: SHE WAS ASKED TO DANCE

1. In describing the people as "sheep without a shepherd," Mark is giving a gentle indictment against the religious leaders who saw themselves as the "shepherds" of the people. The term *compassion* is translated as "his heart went out to them" in the Revised English Bible. This is an excellent explanation of compassion.
2. Jesus was quoting from Hosea 6:6.
3. See John 6.

CHAPTER 2: "NEITHER DO I CONDEMN YOU"

1. R. Alan Culpepper, *The Gospel and Letters of John* (Nashville: Abingdon Press, 1998), 170.
2. John A. Sanford, *Mystical Christianity: A Psychological Commentary on the Gospel of John* (New York: Crossroad Publishing Company, 1993), 168.
3. Eugene H. Peterson, "What's Wrong with Spirituality?" *Christianity Today*, 42, no.8, 52.
4. See Genesis 3:12.
5. See Exodus 23:1, 7.

CHAPTER 3: "THE OTHER NINE, WHERE ARE THEY?"

1. The journey section ends as Jesus approaches the outskirts of Jerusalem. See Luke 19:28.
2. Michael Wilcock, *The Message of Luke* (Downers Grove, IL: Inter-Varsity Press, 1979), 158.

3. It is probable that Samaritans' ethnicity had some roots in the Jewish race. Jews who did not go into Babylonian captivity married foreigners who had settled in the land. Their descendants became known as Samaritan.
4. A primary criterion for determining an outcast concerned the understanding and knowledge of the Law. Those ignorant of the Law were considered outcasts.
5. See Leviticus 13:45-46. The term *leprous disease* could refer to a variety of skin diseases; it does not necessarily refer to our modern day leprosy.

Chapter 4: Ignored

1. I have chosen to focus on Matthew's account since only he highlights that Jesus ignored the woman. See also Mark's account (7:24-30).
2. Mark, not Matthew, makes this point in Mark 7:25.
3. Abraham Heschel, *Quest for God: Studies in Prayer and Symbolism,* vol. 1 (New York: Crossroad Publishing Company, 1954), 34.
4. "Sir" is the translation used in the Revised English Bible.
5. See John 8:1-12 and also chapter 2 of this book.
6. Eugene H. Peterson, *Praying with Jesus* (San Francisco: HarperSanFrancisco, 1993), entry for May 19.

Chapter 5: The Man Who Did Not Want to Be Healed

1. Lesslie Newbigin, *The Light Has Come* (Grand Rapids: William B. Eerdmans Publishing Company, 1982), 63.
2. Culpepper, 150.
3. Sanford, 132.
4. Newbigin, 62.
5. Sanford, 134.

Chapter 6: At the End of the Day

1. Henri J. M. Nouwen, *Making All Things New* (Dublin, Ireland: Gill and Macmillan, 1982), 24.

Chapter 7: "Who Touched Me?"

1. See also Matthew 8:18-26 and Luke 8:40-48. Unless otherwise indicated, I will follow the story from Mark's account.
2. William L. Lane, *The Gospel of Mark* (Grand Rapids: William B. Eerdmans Publishing Company, 1974), 192.
3. Lane, 190.
4. See Matthew 15:21-28. See also chapter 4 of this book.
5. David Gooding, *According to Luke* (Grand Rapids: William B. Eerdmans Publishing Company, 1987), 149.
6. See John 5:19, where Jesus asserts that he can do nothing by himself, but only as "the Father" wills.
7. Lane, 193.
8. Donald English, *The Message of Mark* (Leicester, England: Inter-Varsity Press, 1987), 114.
9. Lane, 192.
10. Ibid., 193.
11. Gooding, 150.
12. John 5:1-18 and chapter 5 of in this book.

Other Resources from Augsburg

Seasons of Friendship by Marjory Zoet Bankson
160 pages, 0-8066-9016-X (current edition, available now)
             0-8066-5136-9 (rev. edition, January 2005)

Traces the cycles of Naomi and Ruth for clues about women's needs for varying friendships in different seasons of life.

Kindred Sisters by Dandi Daley Mackall
160 pages, 0-8066-2828-6

The stories of Elizabeth, Mary, Anna, Mary Magdalene, Salome, Pilate's wife, and others invite meditation and reflection on contemporary issues of life and faith. Each story includes biblical references, a prayer, and activities that make New Testament women come alive.

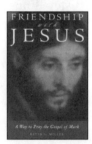

Friendship with Jesus by David L. Miller
176 pages, 0-8066-3894-X

This guide and workbook helps readers to actually experience events recorded in the Gospel of Mark, so that biblical times, places, and people come to life vividly. As the events unfold before the reader's eyes, God's revelation becomes a present event, and Jesus becomes a companion and friend.

Spirited Women by Mary Ellen Ashcroft
128 pages, 0-8066-4027-8

Combining biblical scholarship, midrash, and an imaginative, fictional approach, Mary Ellen Ashcroft takes a new look at seven biblical women: Mary Magdalene, Maria, Mary the Mother of Jesus, Joanna, The Samaritan Woman, and Martha.

Available wherever books are sold.